The Prison Industrial Complex:

Race, Crime & Justice in New York

by John Flateau

DUBOIS BUNCHE CENTER FOR PUBLIC POLICY

MEDGAR EVERS COLLEGE C.U.N.Y.
DR. EDISON O. JACKSON, PRESIDENT

Dedication

This work is dedicated to America's young Black and Latino men and women, and to their legislators, institutions, communities and families whose courageous leadership is critical, in order to protect, preserve and develop our future.

"The spirit of the Lord God is upon me; because the Lord hath anointed me to preach good tidings unto the meek; he hath sent me to bind up the broken-hearted, to proclaim liberty to the captives, and the opening of the prison to them that are bound.

To proclaim the acceptable year of the Lord, and the day of vengeance of our God; to comfort all that mourn...

And they shall build the old waste, they shall raise up the former desolations, and they shall repair the waste cities, the desolations of many generations."

Isaiah 61: 1-2, 4

Published by

Medgar Evers College Press
The DuBois Bunche Center for Public Policy
Medgar Evers College, City University of New York
1650 Bedford Ave., Rm. 2032C
Brooklyn, New York 11225

Cover and book design by
John Flateau and Thomas R. Paisley IV

Lithographic production coordination and art direction by
Thomas R. Paisley IV for Destiny Universal, Inc.

Cover photo by
Michael Littlejohn for Creative Images, Inc.

Library of Congress Catalog Card Number: 96-83258
ISBN 1-888085-00-2 (pbk.)

First edition 1996

Acknowledgements

Dr. Edison O. Jackson, the President of Medgar Evers College, CUNY is the founder and Chairman of the Board of Advisors of the DuBois Bunche Center for Public Policy (DBC), a university-based think tank, specializing in urban policy issues which impact upon communities of color. President Jackson's vision and material support make the work of the DuBois Bunche Center possible. The support and encouragement of the DBC Board of Advisors has been invaluable. (See Appendix B.) Hon. Edward Griffith, Assistant Speaker of the New York State Assembly, along with the Brooklyn delegation of state legislators provided DBC support, through state grants administered by the N.Y.S. Education Department and the CUNY Research Foundation. This is one of several policy studies produced by the DuBois Bunche Center.

Dr. Robert B. Lee, Dr. Carlos Russell and Dr. Obesegun Awolabi, provided early direction to the DuBois Bunche Center, assisted by William H. Boone III, Amir Al -Islam, Jennette Ryan and student interns. Dean Arthur Taylor and Dean Tom Oliver; Dr. Betty Shabbaz and Dr. Mary Umolu; MEC Center directors Dr. Esmeralda Simmons, Dr. George Irish and Safiya Bandele have been very supportive of DBC intiatives. We are grateful to N.Y.S. Supreme Court Justice Lewis Douglass and Zeke Clement for their participation in a DBC Criminal Justice Symposium with faculty, students and community leaders, which helped frame key issues in this report. Former DBC researcher Dr. Monica Gordon made significant contributions to this report. Mark Pollard, Esq., Greg Mayers, DBC Deputy Director, and Richard Green also provided insightful comments and recommendations. We gratefully acknowledge the editorial assistance of Adele Flateau in producing this publication.

The Author...

John Flateau is the Executive Director of the DuBois Bunche Center for Public Policy at Medgar Evers College; and a faculty member in the Public Administration Department. He is the former Chief of Staff to Mayor David Dinkins; Senior Vice President of the N.Y.S. Urban Development Corporation and Executive Director of the N.Y.S. Black and Puerto Rican Legislative Caucus, Inc. He is pursuing a Ph.D. in Political Science at the Graduate Center, City University of New York; holds a Master's degree in Public Administration from Baruch College, CUNY; and holds a B.A. degree from New York University. He is a generalist with an extensive background in the public policy and public administration arenas, including work in the criminal justice field.

The opinions expressed in this report are solely those of the author, and do not necessarily reflect the opinions of the DuBois Bunche Center, its Board of Advisors, Medgar Evers College, or the City University of New York.

Table of Contents

DBC

DuBois Bunche Center for Public Policy   **MEDGAR EVERS COLLEGE, C.U.N.Y.**

Appendix B: Information Section   111

The DuBois Bunche
Center for Public Policy

The Board of Advisors

List of Tables

List of Figures

I. Introduction:

A Prison Industrial Complex?

Dwight David Eisenhower was born in Denison, Texas in 1890. He graduated from the U.S. Military Academy at West Point in 1915, and was commissioned as an infantry officer. He went on to become a legendary American hero, with a military career spanning four decades, including Allied Supreme Commander in World War II; and Supreme Commander of the NATO forces after the war. Mainly because of his distinguished military record, he was drafted and popularly elected the 34th President of the United States, serving two terms from 1953 through 1960. [1]

On January 17, 1961 in his farewell address to the nation, President Eisenhower delivered what many would consider a chilling commentary on the U.S. military, corporate and academic sectors-- and this, coming from a pre-eminent military leader and former President of Columbia University. Eisenhower warned the American people that the Soviet Union and the Cold War were not the only threats to our democracy. He warned that the "military industrial complex," as he termed it, was also a major threat, stating:

---

[1] Edward M. Coffman, "Dwight David Eisenhower," Encarta, Microsoft Corp. and Funk & Wagnall's Corp. 1994.

"In the councils of Government, we must guard against the acquisition of unwarranted influence, whether sought or unsought by the military-industrial complex. The potential for the disastrous rise of misplaced power persists and will exist.

"We must never let the weight of this combination endanger our liberties or democratic processes. We should take nothing for granted. Only an alert and knowledgeable citizenry can compel the proper meshing of the huge industrial and military defense with our peaceful methods and goals, so that security and liberty may prosper together." [2]

Using the term "military industrial complex," Eisenhower was referring to the potent combination of the U.S. military establishment; the corporate sector, including the massive armaments industry in particular; the academic sector which conducted significant research and development for the military; and the federal government, which included heavily funded defense and security agencies, as well as key executive branch and congressional leadership, in defense, national security and foreign affairs.

One can draw a number of parallels between the military industrial complex and a so called "prison industrial complex." There are massive economic and political interests vested in the prison industrial complex in terms of business and employment components of prison construction, contractual services, and inmate

---

[2] Fred J. Cook, *The Warfare State*, Collier Books, New York, 1969. pp.11-13.

maintenance and supervision operations. It involves all three branches of government: the executive branch, in terms of prison and law enforcement administration; the legislative branch, in terms of defining and drafting criminal laws and sanctions; and the judicial branch, in terms of sanctioning and applying criminal laws, and conducting trials and sentencing.

Further, the prison industrial complex is driven by the moral and civic imperative of "fighting crime," with a seemingly sacrosanct and unlimited war chest; just as "fighting communism," in an earlier era, had a similar moral imperative and blank check, in terms of resources. As Eisenhower warned of the military industrial complex, an unchecked growing prison industrial complex poses a fundamental threat to democracy and freedom for Black and Latino Americans in particular, as well as for Americans in general.

The prison industrial complex has become by result, if not by intent, an institutionally racist tool of destruction, tacitly sanctioned by the tyranny and silence of the majority. It is overwhelmingly and effectively neutralizing young Black and Latino American males. The outcomes spell devastation for Black and Latino communities; but also a spiritual devastation for the broader America as well. Some argue that the German national soul was condemned because too many "good" Germans claimed they didn't know; knew but failed to oppose; or actually approved and participated in the Jewish Holocaust. With some parallels to what seems to be happening to Black and Latino youth in America today, in Hitler's Germany, the Jewish people were demonized, criminalized and dehumanized; which

DBC

DuBois Bunche Center for Public Policy   MEDGAR EVERS COLLEGE, C.U.N.Y.

set the stage for the extermination process.

Judging by their history of insurrection and struggle against oppression, Africans in America today - the 35 million survivors of a three hundred year African holocaust,- are not likely to sit silently by while the seed of their race is being plucked from their midst, to be ground up in a prison industrial complex. The rise of the prison indusrial complex should be a cause for alarm, not just throughout Black and Latino America, but throughout all of America.

America must stop the violence now -- the internal violence plaguing communities of color, and the institutional violence which is destroying our youth. If today, we allow America's millions of young Black and Latino males to become just so much grist for a prison industrial complex, then we have killed our future.

Then other burdens of, and dangers to, society will take their place on tomorrow's list of extermination. Martin Luther King, Jr. and others have observed, that the destiny and freedom of all Americans are inextricably woven together; and that an oppressor loses their own freedom in seeking to constrain the freedom of others. If we don't join together to stop the madness, then we will hang separately.

This report is about race, crime, and justice, and a conceptual framework for viewing these forces as interlocking phenomena, which have insidiously converged to profoundly impact upon communities of color. This report borrows from the concept of the "military industrial complex," as a conceptual tool for understanding major elements of the criminal justice system, how and why they are interrelated, and the terrible outcomes which they generate.

Following chapters of this report discuss in greater depth, the issues raised in this overview. Chapter II discusses the magnitude and impacts of the criminal justice system upon Black and Latino communities. Chapter III explores how race, the historical criminalization of Blacks, and the perception of crime are driving the build-up of the prison industrial complex. Chapter IV looks at key symptoms of institutional racism in the judicial branch. Chapter V looks at the political economy of the criminal justice system -- an economy built upon Black and Latino commodities of exchange. Chapter VI looks at recent trends in federal and state crime legislation and how these trends are feeding the build-up of the prison industrial complex. Chapter VII proposes solutions and policy recommendations to address the problem of a prison industrial complex which is devastating Black and Latino communities in New York and across America. Appendix A contains tables and figures which constitute a wealth of data on racial, geographic and other dimensions of the inmate recidivism problem in New York. Appendix B contains the history, mission, goals and activities of the DuBois Bunche Center; and lists its Board of Advisors.

II. The Prison Industrial Complex:

Black & Latino Community Impacts

Perception is reality. This conventional wisdom has no more profound manifestation than with regard to the issue of crime. Crime reports from the Federal Bureau of Investigation and the New York City Police Department unequivocally indicate that crime has been on a downward trend in New York City and elsewhere, for the past three years. There were 385 less murders and 13,000 less robberies in New York City in 1994 than in 1993.[3] Nonetheless, in the public perception, crime continues to be a major issue of concern. Many politicians, legislators, criminal justice officials and the media, appear to play more to the public perception of crime, than to dealing with viable responses to the reality of crime, which is declining.

In the past fifteen years, the total U.S. prison population has doubled to 1.5 million. From 1972-1994, New York's prison inmate population has quintupled from 12,500 to 68,000, with an additional 53,000 released on parole. (See Figure 1.) The N.Y.C. Probation

---

[3] See Fox Butterfield, "Serious Crimes Fall for Third Year, but Experts Warn Against Seeing Trend," *New York Times*. May 23, 1995. Page A14. Based on *F.B.I. Uniform Crime Reports, 1994*, released in May 1995.

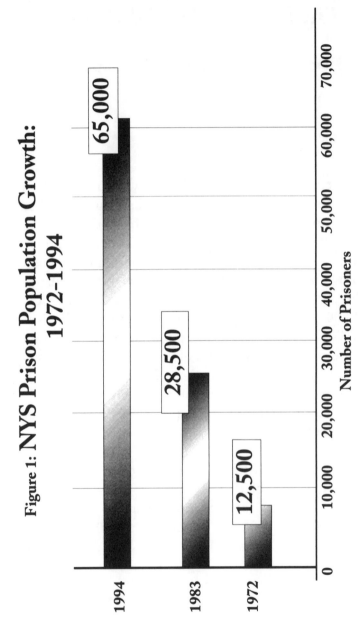

Figure 1: NYS Prison Population Growth: 1972-1994

Sources: NYS Dept. of Correctional Services & Correctional Association of New York data.

Department supervises an additional 80,000 adults and 4,000 youth[4]. The N.Y.C. Corrections Department holds at any one time nearly 20,000 detainees, and over 100,000 detainees per year pass through Riker's Island and borough detention centers. These are individuals who are not yet convicted of a crime. These numbers cumulatively exceed 250,000 and the vast majority of inmates are Black and Latino males between the ages of 18 and 39, from just a few New York City communities: Central Brooklyn, Lower East Side, northern Manhattan, the South Bronx and Southeast Queens. Blacks and Latinos are 49% of the city population but over 92% of the city inmates. They are 23% of the state population and over 85% of the state inmates.[5] (See Figures 2 and 3, and Table 1.)

With massive and growing numbers of prisoners and declining crime rates, one would think that these trends would be interpreted as breakthroughs which address and solve the crime problem in New York City, New York State and beyond. However, the policy trend at the federal, state and local levels seems strictly geared towards incarceration, which is mainly a reactive response to crime. There are policy trends to expand definitions of criminality; de-emphasize crime prevention, youth development, delinquency prevention, and drug treatment; and a total neglect of funding to address crime generative factors such as chronic inner city unem-

---

[4] "Community Corrections," Atlas Of Crime And Justice In New York City. Vera Institute Of Justice. 1993. p.52

[5] Sources: U.S. Bureau of the Census, Population Reports; "Statistical and Narrative Summary, Executive Budget, SFY 1995-96," Assembly Ways and Means Committee; N.Y.S. Department Of Corrections; N.Y.C. Department Of Correction.

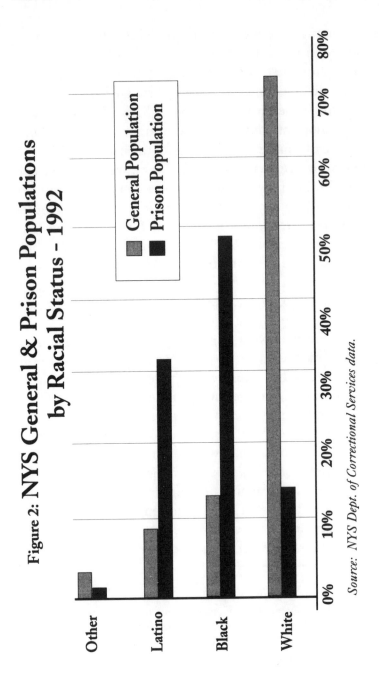

Figure 2: NYS General & Prison Populations by Racial Status – 1992

Source: NYS Dept. of Correctional Services data.

ployment and educational failure.

One construct of these crime control approaches, which has major impetus at the national, state and local levels, reflects the following logic. To solve the crime problem, one should expand the definitions of criminality; increase the severity of punishment; lock up a maximum number of criminals for a maximum period; and society will be safe again from those people who commit the crimes. This is a bipartisan view widely shared by minorities, New Yorkers and probably most Americans.

This crime-solving approach appears sound and politically correct to many, in small town, suburban and rural white America, as well as urban America. However, this solution ignores several critical issues for the Central Brooklyns, the Harlems, the South Bronxes and the Southeast Queens' of America, such as: racism in the criminal justice system; the political economy of the prison industrial complex and the lives which it is built upon; and the ravaging impacts of crime and punishment on individuals, families and communities of color.

The dominant society's crime solution spells a terrible devastation and dilemma for Black America, for Watts, the South Side, Harlem, Morrisania, Jamaica, East New York, Brownsville and Bedford-Stuyvesant. For a "punishment only," narrowly defined crime solution, as much as the destructive spiral of crime itself, is translating into an unacceptable, intolerable decimation of communities and people of African descent, with a particular targeting of young Black males. Society's crime problems and solutions are defined along racial lines and in Black communities, the effects of crime and

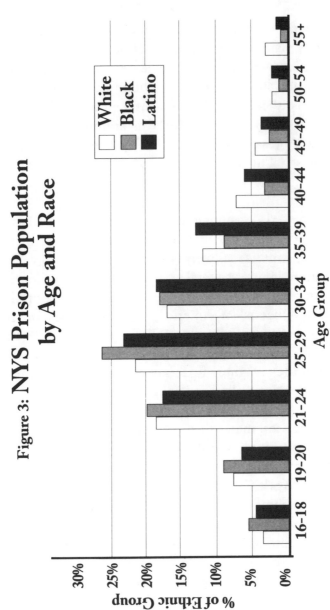

Figure 3: NYS Prison Population by Age and Race

Source: NYS Dept. of Correctional Services data.

punishment cut deeply across class lines, impacting the poor, working class and middle class communities.

Black people hate crime perhaps more than any other group, in large measure because they are victimized by crime more than any other group. Because of their visceral experience, Black people want criminals to be locked up as much as any other group. However, part of their dilemma is that many of the Black males accused of committing crimes are the cousins, uncles, fathers, sons, boyfriends, husbands, friends, associates and neighbors of people who live in the Black community.

High numbers of criminal Black males mean that high numbers of Black families and communities are negatively impacted. Crime solutions which broaden the net of Black incarceration and criminalization will exact increasingly intolerable human, social and economic costs upon the Black community and the larger society. It also raises serious questions about the Black community's own ability to properly raise, guide and control its young males. If white America is more than willing to pay the price of a solution as it defines one, it would be suicide for Black America to endorse those same prescriptions.

Deteriorating socio-economic conditions in the Black community, heavily driven by educational failure, joblessness and public sector budget cuts, are increasingly excarbating the crime problem. If these trends continue unabated, then the ratio of young Black males in many Black communities, who are associated with the criminal justice system may escalate from 1 in 4, to 1 in 2, or higher. Crime generative factors and their impacts

Table 1: NYS General and Prison Populations by Racial Status – 1992

	Whites		Blacks		Latinos		Other	
Prison Pop.	9,100	14.0%	32,500	50.0%	22,880	35.2%	520	0.8%
General Pop.	13.5 mill.	74.4%	2.2 mill.	12.4%	2.0 mill.	10.8%	0.4 mill.	2.4%

Sources: U.S. Bureau of Census and NYS Dept. of Correctional Services data.

are already at untolerably high levels throughout Black communities, with further desperation being generated by massive federal, state and city budget cuts to vital health and welfare programs and services which constitute a critical underpinning and safety net for the Black community infrastructure.

Most national, state and local criminal justice policymakers have a disadvantaged perspective from the outside looking in, with respect to Black America's social, economic, criminal justice issues and problems of concern. Because of this handicap, policymakers have a limited capacity to understand the internal dynamics of the Black community, in relation to these serious issues and problems. With radically alien political and ideological imperatives, the current regimes of policymakers are not interested in 'understanding' the problem, but rather, in solving it their way. If we're not careful, however, one group's 'final solution,' may end up becoming another group's genocide.

Central Brooklyn Pipeline

There is a complex web of social, economic and governmental factors, with roots internal and external to Central Brooklyn and similar communites, which seem to converge into a mechanism known as the criminal justice system. Notwithstanding, that human beings should be held accountable for their actions, this system seems to be engulfing young Black and Latino males, and siphoning them right out of their communities and into a criminal justice 'pipeline.' The main funnel or entry point for this pipeline is a small and critical group

of Black and Latino neighborhoods, dominated by
Central Brooklyn, the largest African diasporan community in North America. Major checkpoints in the
pipeline are the Police Department (criminal apprehension), the District Attorney's Office (prosecution) and
the courts (trial, conviction and sentencing). There are
discriminatory diversion options for white detainees who
are steered out of the pipeline but little such considera-
tion for black and brown detainees who are propelled
forward in the pipeline, flooding an alarmingly disproportionate number of Black and Latino males into our
state prisons (85%) and city jails (92%).

Most criminal justice strategies and policies have
focused on the 'middle passage,' and the back end of the
pipeline, with questionable results: tougher laws to
define and catch more criminals; a multi-billion dollar
prison building program to hold more criminals; and
from the advocates, improving prison living conditions.
In a single decade from the early 1980s to present, New
York City and State governments committed over $ 4
billion on new prison construction and expansion; spent
billions more on prisoner maintenance and operations,
more courts and more police; and tripled state prison
capacity to nearly 70,000. This does not include city and
county jail figures. According to a recent study by the
Sentencing Project on international incarceration rates,
New York and America have higher incarceration rates
for Black males than South Africa. New York State and
City Budget reports for Fiscal Year 1995-96, along with a
recent Vera Institute study, indicate that the combined
New York State and New York City criminal justice system is approximately a $5 billion a year industry.
Congress and state and local legislatures are broadening

criminal statutes to define, apprehend and jail more criminals. Federal, state and city governments are decreasing spending on health, education and welfare while increasing spending on criminal justice. There is an unmistakable correlation between the two trends. However the public perception, reinforced heavily by the media, is that crime is rampant while in reality it is declining.

The past and present configurations of strategies and allocations of resources have clearly failed to solve the crime problem. Indeed, some might question if there is real policy intent to solve the problem. Actual resolution of the crime problem would cripple a major industry and put thousands of judges, lawyers and law enforcement personnel out of work and cripple upstate economies. The rulers of the vast criminal justice enterprise have a conflict of interest in solving the crime problem, just as some argue that the welfare bureaucracy has a conflict of interest in getting people off of welfare.

The vested interest of Central Brooklyn and other Black and Latino communities of this nation is to implement real, long-term solutions to the crime problem. Their public policy agenda is not to fix up and expand the criminal justice pipeline -- but to pursue strategies to shrink it, dismantle it, to shut it down -- and prevent the pipeline from further siphoning present and future generations of Black and Latino youth. These communities must bear the responsibility for raising youth who will possess the positive values of spirituality, self-esteem, family and community. At the same time, doers in any society must pay the consequences of illegal actions.

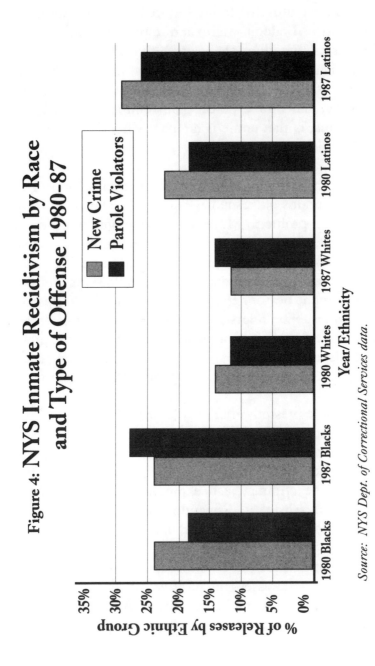

Figure 4: **NYS Inmate Recidivism by Race and Type of Offense 1980-87**

Source: NYS Dept. of Correctional Services data.

John Henrik Clarke and other scholars argue that, to this day, neither Africa nor her diasporan children have yet recovered from the holocaust of the slave trade, chattel slavery, racism and colonialism. Today, failing public education, lack of economic opportunity, and the triple plagues of violence, guns and drugs is wreaking havoc and spilling the lifeblood of the Central Brooklyns of this nation. Metaphorically, the criminal justice pipeline is like a slave ship, transporting human cargo along interstate triangular trade routes from Black and Brown communities; through the middle passage of police precincts, holding pens, detention centers and courtrooms; to upstate or downstate jails; back to communities as unrehabilitated escapees; and back to jail in a vicious recidivist cycle. (See Figure 4, Table 2 and Appendix A.)

As we shall discuss in the next chapter, the public perceives crime as a top social problem currently facing the nation. Within the last thirty years, the nation has shifted from concerns with the civil rights movement and social justice, to a focus on criminal justice. The focus of the criminal justice system has been on controlling 'street crimes,' which are classified as crimes against the person (rape, robbery, assault and homicide). Black and Latino males have been the primary target of this policy shift especially since the 1970s.

Blacks and Latinos in Prisons

The Correctional Association of New York reported in 1994 that there were over 65,000 persons in New York State prisons, up from 12,500 in 1972 and

Table 2: NYS Inmate Recidivism: by Race & Type of Offense, 1987

1987	Releases	Recidivists		Type of Offense			
				New Crimes		Parole Violators	
Blacks	5,909	3,107	52.6%	1,496	25.3%	1,831	31.0%
Whites	2,825	866	30.7%	416	14.7%	452	16.0%
Latinos	4,215	2,483	58.9%	1,285	30.5%	1,178	27.9%
Other	50	14	28.0%	5	10.0%	9	18.0%
Total	12,999	6,470	49.8%	3,202	24.6%	3,470	26.7%

Source: NYS Dept. of Correctional Services data.

28,500 in 1983 which is 500% since 1972 and over 228% since 1983. This rapid escalation in the prison population is the consequence of the mandatory sentencing requirements of the 1973 Rockefeller Drug Law which require harsh prison terms for the possession or sale of even relatively small amounts of drugs; and the Second Felony Offender Law which requires prison terms for all repeat felons regardless of the nature of the offense or the background or motivation of the offender. Over 90% of all prison inmates are imprisoned for drug offenses. Of this population in New York State prisons, 50% of all prisoners are African-American, and 32% are Latino.

The arrest and incarceration of Blacks and Latinos increased dramatically in New York City jails and in New York State prisons, since the 1970s. The leading causes of arrests during the 1980s were: drug sales and drug possession. (See Figure 5.) All arrests increased for all racial/ ethnic categories, but there was a great racial disparity in arrests. The rate of increase for Blacks was 95%, Latinos, 146% and whites only 36%. Arrests for drug sales increased by 320%, 697%, and 54% for Blacks, Latinos, and whites, respectively. Arrests for drug possession increased by 229%, 371% and 225% for Blacks, Latinos, and whites, respectively.

By 1990, the two leading causes of arrest for Black males were drug possession and larceny; for Latinos, drug sales and drug possession; and for whites, drug possession and assault. Following is a profile of trends for Blacks and Latinos in the criminal justice system. In 1960, Black men were 41% of the New York State prison population; white men were 48%; and Latinos were 10%. A generation later, in 1990, Black men were 51%

Figure 5: Incarceration for Violent Crimes versus Drug Offenses: 1983 and 1993

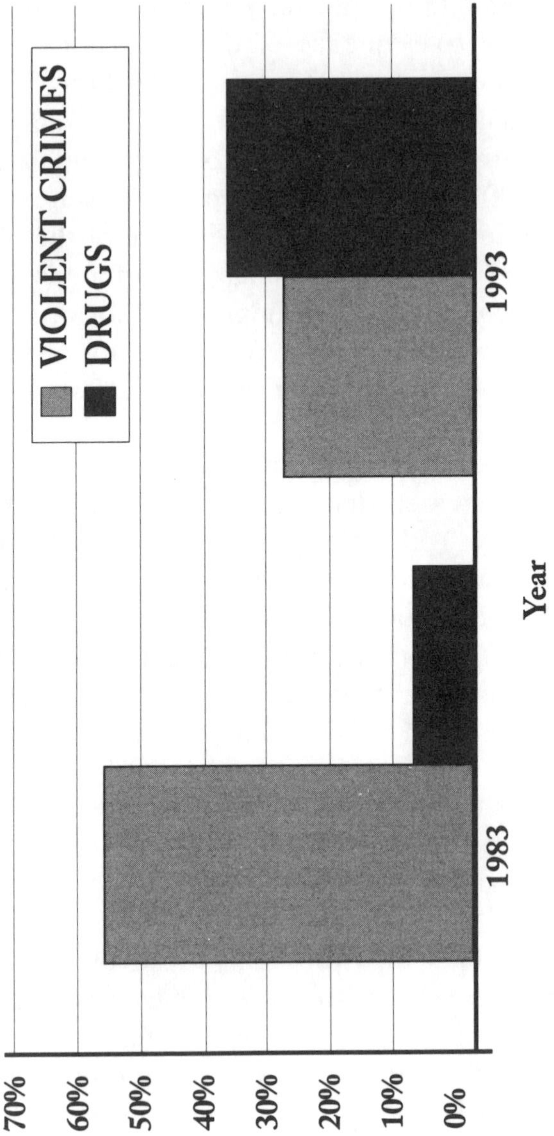

VIOLENT CRIMES
DRUGS

70%
60%
50%
40%
30%
20%
10%
0%

1983

1993

Year

Source: NYS Dept. of Correctional Services data.

of the state prison inmates; Latinos were 32%; and whites were only 17%. White prisoners declined from 48% to 17%; while Black and Latino prisoners increased from 51% to 83%, a 63% increase. By 1993, Blacks were still 51%, Latinos 32%, and whites further declined to only 14% of the state prison population. Yet, Blacks and Latinos are only 12.4% and 10.8% of the State's general population, according to the 1990 Census. (See Figure 2.)

In 1993 there were 65,000 persons in New York State prisons, a 500% increase since 1972, when there were 12,000 state prisoners. Blacks and Latinos are 85% of the state prison population; and 93% of inmates in New York City. In the New York City Correctional facilities, Black men made up 57% and Latino males 36% of all inmates, thus New York City's inmate population is 93% Black and Latino in a city that is 49% Black and Latino. White males made up only 6 percent of the city inmate population..

A majority of state inmates have a history of drug abuse problems. Blacks are 47% and Latinos 46% of drug offenders in New York State prisons. Whites are only 6% of imprisoned drug offenders, despite studies showing that whites constitute a major proportion of drug users and sellers. There were 3,529 women, only 5% of New York State prison inmate population. Black women are 54 %, Latino women 35%, and white women only 11% of the female inmate population. Black and Latino women represent 93% of the female drug offenders in New York State prisons; and white women make up only 6% of this category.

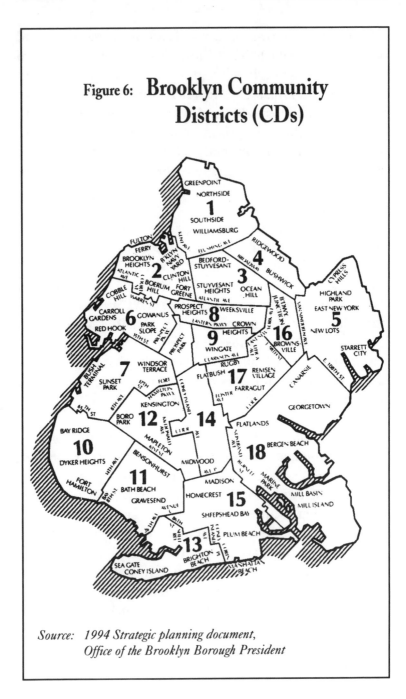

Figure 6: **Brooklyn Community Districts (CDs)**

*Source: 1994 Strategic planning document,
Office of the Brooklyn Borough President*

Seventy-five percent (75%) of all prison inmates did not graduate from high school or earn a high school equivalency diploma. Sixty percent (60%) of all offenders sent to prison in 1993 were convicted for non-violent crimes. Forty-two percent (42%) of inmates are serving time for first felony convictions. Although crime has decreased in New York City, it appears that the unofficial policy of some politicians and the media has been to maintain high levels of fear concerning crime. Arrest rates remain consistently high for the central Brooklyn area. Six of the top ten Community Districts citywide, ranking highest in crime are in Central Brooklyn. (See Figure 6.) East New York (CD 5), served by the 75th Precinct, ranked number one on the FBI's Uniform Crime Report. (See Table 3.) Also, foreign-born blacks, specifically, young Caribbean immigrant males, are increasingly populating the city jails and the state prison system.[6] These communities all have very high incidences of what sociologists define as "crime generative factors" (i.e. poor socioeconomic conditions).

Police Corruption and Brutality

Volumes have already been written about police corruption and brutality in the Black and Latino community. In 1991, The Center for Law and Social Justice at Medgar Evers College, issued a report entitled "Police and Racial Violence: Fact Versus Fiction," which documented a pattern of police violence in Black and Latino neighborhoods. More recently, in 1994, The Mollen

---

[6] See, Yolande Forde, "Caribbean People Under the Control of the Criminal Justice System in New York State." Caribbean Research Center, Medgar Evers College. 1995.

Table 3: Brooklyn & NYC Precinct Rankings - Crimes Against Persons

	January - June 1994				January - December 1993		
Rank	Precinct	CD	Neighborhood	Rank	Precinct	CD	Neighborhood
1	75	5	(B'klyn - East New York)	1	75	5	(B'klyn - East N.Y.)
2	44	4	(Bronx)	2	67	17	(B'klyn - East Flatbush)
3	67	17	(B'klyn - East Flatbush)	3	77	8	(B'klyn - Crown Hgts.)
4	79	3	(B'klyn - Bedford/Stuyvesant)	4	73	16	(B'klyn - Brownsville)
5	43	9	(Bronx)	5	44	4	(Bronx)
6	46	5	(Bronx)	6	79	3	(B'klyn - Bed-Stuy)
7	73	16	(B'klyn - Brownsville)	7	46	5	(Bronx)
8	77	8	(B'klyn - Crown Heights)	8	43	9	(Bronx)
9	34	12	(Manhattan)	9	40	1	(Bronx)
10	14	4,5	(Manhattan)	10	14	4,5	(Manhattan)

Sources: "FBI Index Crimes - URC (Uniform Crime Report)" and
- *Computer Information Services, NYC Department of City Planning data.*

Commission, appointed by former Mayor David Dinkins, released a report which documented widespread and systemic patterns of police corruption, brutality and abuse of authority in several police precincts covering Black and Latino neighborhoods throughout New York City.

An April 9, 1995 Newsday article entitled, "New York's Roughest?"[7] reports that according to the independent Civilian Complaint Review Board (CCRB), in 1994, Mayor Giuliani's first year in office, police brutality allegations increased 40%. Overall citizen complaints against police for excessive force, abuse of authority, offensive language and discourtesy, increased 37%, from 5,597 to 7,659 or an increase of 2,062 complaints. Sixty-eight percent (68%) of these complaints were from people not arrested, and not at the scene of an arrest. By comparison, in Mayor Dinkins' first year in office, there were 3,377 complaints, according to the 1990 Annual Report of the Civilian Complaint Investigative Bureau (CCIB), a unit of the Police Department.[8] The 1990 numbers might have been artificially low, since the CCIB was attached to the Police Department and the CCRB is not. Nonetheless, there was a 227% increase in complaints against police, comparing Dinkins' and Giuliani's first years in office.

Further symptoms of a police force potentially out of control have included recent public incidents.

---

[7] William Rashbaum and Juan Forero, "New York's Roughest?" Newsday, April 9, 1995. p.A6; and "Top Cop Nixed Brutality Unit Idea: Sources." p.A8.

[8] CLSJ Report, pp.15-16.

There was a 1993 Anti-Dinkins rally at City Hall, with
then Patrolmen's Benevolent Association endorsed mayoral candidate Rudolph Giuliani addressing several hundred unruly off duty officers, some of whom insulted
Black City Council members in the City Hall parking
lot.   In 1995, there were several rampaging N.Y.P.D.
police officers, at a number of Washington D.C. hotels,
while they were in town for a national memorial ceremo-
ny for slain police officers.   Police Commissioner
William Bratton has publicly acknowledged that there
are alcohol, drug and discipline problems on the police
force.

Some in the Black and Latino community view
the police as a foreign army of occupation, with some jus-
tification: nearly 50% of New York City's police force
does not live in New York City, but in the surrounding
suburbs. Cultural and racial diversity of New York City's
police force is still a major problem for a world class city
that is 56% non-white and has over 100 different cultures
and ethnicities.   In a 1993 public hearing before the
city's Equal Employment Practices Commission,
NYPD's Personnel Chief O'Sullivan noted that the force
of over 30,000 police officers is 73% white, 11% Black
and 14% Latino; and that 16 out of 17 psychologists on
the applicant interview team were white.

Thus Blacks and Latinos aspiring to become one
of "New York's Finest" face several hurdles. First, a disproportionate number have prior contact with the criminal justice system, which might disqualify them from
employment; or background problems which are a low
investigative priority for NYPD. Applicants are required

to take a written exam, which Black and Latino police fraternal organizations have successfully challenged as discriminatory.[9] Furthermore, minority applicants are often psychologically screened out by a battery of nearly all white psychologists. Thus New York City ranks number 50 out of the 50 largest cities in America, with an Equal Employment Opportunity (EEO) Index for Black police officers, according to a recent University of Nebraska study.[10]

New York City Crime Trends: Up in the 1980s -- Down in the 1990s

The single most important cause of the rise in violent crime in the 1980s was the crack and drug epidemic. It drove street crimes committed by drug addicts to support their habits. And it drove brutal turf wars by drug cartels and their local distributors and enforcers seeking to control a local market share of the international, multibillion dollar drug industry. Violent crimes increased by 23% in New York City between 1985 and 1989, and the murder rate increased by 35%. Brooklyn, the most populous borough, also had the highest percentage of complaints and arrests consistently throughout this period, followed by the Bronx, Manhattan, Queens and Staten Island (Annual Report on Social

---

[9] EEPC 1993 Annual Report, pp.24-27; and Appendix B, Summary of Case Citations, Guardians Assoc. v. Civil Service Commission et. al.
[10] EEPC 1993 Annual Report, pp.28-31; Samuel Walker and K.B. Turner, "A Decade of Modest Progress: Employment of Black and Hispanic Police Officers, 1983-1992," Dept. of Criminal Justice, University of Nebraska at Omaha. October 1993.

Table 4: Analysis of New Inmates by Age (16-34yrs.), Gender and Race – 1992

Age	Total	Male	Female	White	Black	Latino
16-18	1,598	1,563	35	152	924	482
	6.5%	6.7%	2.6%	4.5%	7.3%	5.4%
19-20	2,154	2,087	67	270	1,171	697
	8.7%	9.0%	4.9%	7.9%	9.3%	7.9%
21-24	5,024	4,773	251	673	2,569	1,718
	20.4%	20.5%	18.4%	19.8%	20.3%	19.4%
25-29	5,756	5,697	59	776	3,301	2,170
	23.4%	24.5%	4.3%	22.8%	26.1%	24.5%
30-34	4,766	4,280	486	631	2,383	1,685
	19.3%	18.4%	35.6%	18.5%	18.9%	19.0%

Source: NYS Dept. of Correctional Services data.

Indicators, 1990, City of New York).

Data for 1990 show continuation of the pattern of increase in violent crimes--murder and robbery. The year 1981, noted as a peak period for crime, showed a total of 725,866 crimes. Comparable figures for 1989 and 1990 are 712,419 and 710,221 respectively -- a slight decrease in the number of crimes (NYC -FBI Index of Crimes, January - December, 1991, Department of City Planning).

Juvenile Crime

Juvenile crimes also increased during the period 1985-89. In 1985 nearly 7,400 juveniles (under 16 years old) were arrested for felony crimes. By 1989 the number had increased to 11,558--an increase of 57%. Again, Brooklyn, the most populous borough, had the largest number of juvenile offenders, 37% of the total arrests in 1989 (Annual Report on Social Indicators, 1990:21).

There has also been a corresponding increase in admission to secure facilities for juveniles from 3,221 to 5,404, an increase of 67.8% admitted to the Spofford Juvenile Center, New York City, in that time period (ibid.Fig 3-7). The New York State Council on Children & Families (1988:150) reported that the juvenile arrest rate in New York City was more than twice as high as the rest of the state--91/1000 compared with 41/1000 for the rest of the state. Youth in the age category 16-20 years are treated as adults for the purpose of criminal prosecution. Youths in that age range represented 28 % of all adults arrested in 1985 and 30% of all adults arrested for Part I Violent Offenses--criminal homicide, rape, rob-

Table 5: Analysis of New Inmates by Age (35-55yrs.), Gender and Race - 1992

Age	Total	Male	Female	White	Black	Latino
35-39	2,847	2,564	283	400	1,315	1,110
	11.6%	11.0%	20.7%	11.7%	10.4%	12.5%
40-44	1,362	1,237	125	229	578	542
	5.5%	5.3%	9.1%	6.7%	4.6%	6.1%
45-49	648	608	40	142	221	275
	2.6%	2.6%	2.9%	4.2%	1.7%	3.1%
50-54	253	237	16	50	97	103
	1.0%	1.0%	1.2%	1.5%	0.8%	1.2%
55+	226	221	5	82	70	70
	0.9%	0.9%	0.4%	2.4%	0.6%	0.8%
TOTAL	24,634	23,267	1,367	3,405	12,629	8,852

Source: NYS Dept. of Correctional Services data.

bery, and aggravated assault.

The arrest of youths 16-20 years in 1985 was disproportionally high in New York City--210,981 compared with 89,965 for the rest of the state. This category also represented 76 % of the arrests for violent youth crimes in that year. These 1985 figures represent an accelerating pattern of arrests since 1975 for youth crimes, continuing to the present time. According to a report by the Correctional Association in New York and New York State Coalition for Criminal Justice, (September 1990): On any given day, Nearly 1 in 4 (23%) young African-American men are under the control of the criminal justice system in New York--two times more than all Black males enrolled full-time in college in New York State. Young African-American males are 23 times more likely to be locked up in New York State than young white men. On any given day, 11% of New York's Black males between the ages of 20-29 are confined in a state prison or local jail, with thousands more on probation, on parole and with outstanding warrants.

Drug offenses are the largest category for Black (47%) and Hispanic (46%) inmates; property crimes are the largest category for whites. The number of incarcerated females is 5% of total inmates. Female inmates are approximately 54% Black, 35% Hispanic and 11% white. Total female inmates decreased from 2,264 in 1991 to 1,888 in 1992. Like males, most female inmates are incarcerated for drug offenses. (See Figure 7.)

DBC

DuBois Bunche Center for Public Policy   MEDGAR EVERS COLLEGE, C.U.N.Y.

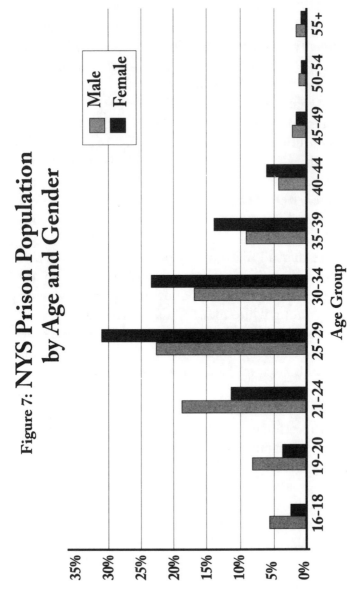

Figure 7: **NYS Prison Population by Age and Gender**

Source: NYS Dept. of Correctional Services data.

During the Dinkins Administration (1990-1993), and continuing through the Giuliani Administration (1994-), there has been a dramatic decline in violent crime, with homicides dropping from over 2,200 to some 1,200 in 1995. This trend is also reflected in other major American cities. There is a major debate as to the causal explanations for New York City's declining crime rates. A partial explanation lies with the Dinkins Administration's Safe Streets Safe City Program, which increased police patrol strength to current levels of 38,000, implemented community policing, and under-wrote large scale youth development services and programs to provide youth with positive options.

The Giuliani Administration's innovative crime control strategies -- including sophisticated tracking of crime incidents and targeted police deployment -- is another factor. Also, criminologists point to demographics -- the aging and increased incarceration of the major age cohorts which commit violent crimes, -- as an important factor. Criminologists also warn of another growing problem: violent juveniles. Unfortunately, the policy solutions to this problem from a Black and Latino community perspective, are very different from those solutions already being implemented by the arbiters of the prison industrial complex: more criminalization and incarceration of Black and Latino youth.

The Giuliani Administration's "quality of life" crime control strategies, while effective in removing societal nuisances (squeegie men, panhandlers etc.), is also further criminalizing thousands of Black and Latino males, as wards of the prison industrial complex.

III. Race, Criminalization & the Perception of Crime

Renowned legal scholar Derrick Bell has observed that:

"Racism in America is much more complex than either the conscious conspiracy of a power elite or the simple delusion of a few ignorant bigots. It is part of our culture. It arises from the assumptions we learn to make about the world, ourselves, and others as well as from the patterns of our fundamental social activities" (Bell, 1987:4-5).

Racism is a major principle of social organization in the United States. It is the historical and institutionalized practice of denying justice to Blacks and other peoples of color. Racism is not static in form, it is continually reconfigured as contemporary society evolves, and its manifestations shift from overt to covert. Bell (1987:5) reminded us that:

"... the task for equal justice advocates have not become simpler because neither slavery's chain nor the lyncher's rope, nor humiliating Jim Crow signs are any longer the main means of holding black people in subordinate status."

DBC

DuBois Bunche Center for Public Policy   MEDGAR EVERS COLLEGE, C.U.N.Y.

The Evolution of Black Criminalization

The American legal system, the foundation and backbone of our democracy, has historically and systematically legislated to criminalize African-Americans since before the founding of the republic. Perhaps the first American statutes to criminalize Blacks were the Slave Codes of the Commonwealth of Virginia, 1680-82. Among their provisions, they made it a crime for Black slaves to have public assemblies, bear arms, travel without their master's permission, or threaten whites. Those crimes were punishable by whippings; and resisting apprehension could result in the death penalty.[11]

Similar Slave Codes were instituted throughout America during the Colonial Period; they were briefly rescinded right after the Civil War; and they were reinstated de facto and de jure, again throughout the Post Reconstruction era. In addition to the above-defined prohibitions which criminalized Blacks, other major Slave Code provisions typically made it a crime for Blacks to learn how to read and write; to sue or testify against a white man; to register and vote; to own land; to hold most jobs and be paid fair market wages; and to be legally married and have children.

Thus, the protection of civil rights and civil liberties under law, which white Americans take for granted, have been an open legal question, or in fact denied to Black people, throughout much of America's history. In the slave owning, founding fathers' Constitution of 1787,

---

[11] Higginbotham, op. cit.

Blacks were not persons but chattel slaves, to be count-
ed as three-fifths of a person. The Missouri
Compromise of 1820, the Kansas Nebraska Act of 1854
and other national legislation was in part about defining
where in America, Blacks would be treated as slaves, and
where in America, they could exercise relatively more
liberty.

In the Dred Scott decision of 1857, the U.S.
Supreme Court reaffirmed the legality of the property
rights of whites to own Blacks as slaves. The
Emancipation Proclamation and the Northern victory in
the Civil War did not end institutional slavery, because
the 13th, 14th and 15th Amendments to the U.S.
Constitution; and the Civil Rights Act of 1875 were still
required to constantly reaffirm the civil rights of Blacks
as free American citizens. In 1876, Republican presi-
dential candidate Rutherford B. Hayes cut one of the
most treacherous political deals in American history. In
order to secure the winning number of Southern Democratic electoral votes, he agreed to withdraw the federal
troops from the South, which were there to protect the
newly acquired civil rights of Black American citizens.

In order to be readmitted to the Union after the
Civil War, the Southern states had to rewrite their constitutions, including the elimination of Slave Code provisions. In most of these states, Blacks who were now free
citizens, registered and voted, played a significant role in
this constitutional drafting process, and Blacks were
elected to many state legislatures and to the U.S.
Congress. After the infamous 'Hayes Compromise' of
1876, the southern states used a reign of terror, with the

Ku Klux Klan in the forefront, in order to disenfranchise Blacks politically, economically and socially from southern society, where 90% of the U.S. Black population resided; and with the full complicity of the federal government.

The southern states then rewrote their state constitutions again, to 'legally' and institutionally disenfranchise Blacks. In 1896, the U.S. Supreme Court decision in Plessy v. Ferguson, reaffirmed and legalized segregation, and signaled assent to the virtual re-enslavement of Blacks.[12] Twentieth century Black America has been engaged in a struggle to regain civil rights established during an all to brief Reconstruction period in the late 19th century. There were many Black civil rights gains in the 1950s and 1960s, including the U.S. Supreme Court's landmark, Brown v. Board of Education decision of 1954 which banned school segregation; the Civil Rights Act of 1964; the Voting Rights Act of 1965 and many other legal and legislative victories which reaffirmed the civil rights of Blacks as American citizens.

Many veterans of those civil rights struggles are now saying that today, the hard fought gains of an earlier era, are now under the threat of extinction, under the hegemony of the current conservative-oriented U.S. Supreme Court; the Republican-controlled 104th Congress; and conservative-controlled state and local governments in New York and around the nation.

Cora Richey Mann (1993), professor of criminal

---

[12] John Hope Franklin, and several other works on Black history.

justice, concluded from her review of the history of law enforcement against racial minorities that minorities rebelled when legal repression became increasingly onerous. The society's response to protests against racially discriminatory practices was to suppress them, with a series of brutal, violent, and lawless acts sanctioned by dominant business and economic interests, the judiciary, law enforcement and the political establishment. When physical repression became counterproductive, Richey Mann, argued:

> "It is at this point in history that racist applications of the criminal law and the resultant incapacitation of minorities through imprisonment became the intensified means of minority control--the current practice. "(1993: 127).

Richey Mann reminded us that the consistent discriminatory application of criminal law against minorities is not a new phenomenon, since federal, state, and local governments have always enacted and enforced laws custom-made for specific racial minority groups. However, criminal law began to be used to warehouse American minorities when the more flagrant, systemic means of economic and political control of minorities used in the past, were no longer feasible or morally acceptable, particularly to the rest of the world.

How did the nation shift from the denial of social justice to Blacks, to criminalizing and incarcerating a significant segment of that population? How is it that Blacks and crime have become so closely associated? Gordon and Beckett are two scholars who attempt to give meaning to this phenomenon. They examine the development of this nation's preoccupation with special types of crimes in recent times. Diane Gordon's (1992) approach is to question the reality of crime. She asked:

> "Do we really have a crime problem? Is it really as bad as many people say it is? What is the nature of our crime problem?"

She concluded that there is a serious crime problem, but it is very complex with several different dimensions. She argues that the politics of the crime problem is to focus on only one aspect of criminal behavior: predatory or street crimes. Public attitudes and public policy are driven by fear of predatory or street crimes, not white collar or organized crimes. The typical white collar or organized crime offender is white; the murder and robbery offenders are presumed to be disproportionally racial minorities. As a consequence, "crime" has been a code word for "Blacks" or "race" in American politics since the mid-1960s.

Beckett (1994) observed that social control issues such as 'street crime' and drug use have received an extraordinary degree of political attention in the United States since 1964. Beckett argues that the state and the mass media play a crucial role in defining and shaping public perception about 'street crime' and drug use. She refers to this as the construction of perception which she defines thusly:

> "Social actors attempt to place issues on the public agenda by calling attention to them and defining them as subject to political action. Furthermore, as advocates of particular kinds of political arrangements and policies, state actors and others represent social issues in ways that imply the need for desired policy outcomes." (Beckett, 1994:426)

Beckett suggested that the focus of the slogan "law and order" which emerged as a response to the civil rights activism in the South in the 1950s, shifted focus to `street crime' during the 1960s. Street crime became associated with social unrest, permissive courts, and declining moral standards. Gordon et. al. (1992:361) observed that public policy of the past 15 years has been dominated by a crime control ideology. Crime, it is argued, can be controlled through tougher law enforcement; more arrests; fewer procedural restraints on police; tougher prosecution; tougher sentencing practices; and greater use of the death penalty. The abject failure of these crime control efforts over the last 15 years has not dampened the public demands for crime control.

The reason for this continuing public demand for crime control, Gordon et. al. suggest, is the way that crime is presented as a social and political issue. Furthermore, they observed that crime is not a 'justice system' problem; that there is an important distinction between crime and disorder as real social phenomena; and that there is persuasive evidence that the level of crime has been directly affected by the social policies of the past decade, and not so much by the criminal justice policies of that period.

"The fear-victimization paradox illustrates the power of street crime on the imagination which, in turn, suggests public susceptibility to political and media manipulation of symbols of crime. Politics channels the expression of fears and dreams."(Gordon et. al. 1992:364).

Gordon claimed that street crimes are highly vulnerable to symbolic politics because political symbols simplify entangled motives, and manipulate the multiplicity of forces that create social pathology.   They reduce complex problems rooted in social and economic structures, and shifting impulses of human nature, to unambiguous representations of good and evil (p.364).

For more than two decades, research has confirmed the fact that the people expressing the greatest fear and anger about street crime are those least likely to be victimized.   The elderly are the most fearful, but are the least victimized.   Women express greater fear than men but are victimized at a lower rate than men.   Whites voice the greatest outrage over crime, but suffer predatory crimes far less than blacks. (Bureau of Justice Statistics, 1991).

Patterns of Discrimination

Are Black and Latino defendants treated differently from whites in the criminal justice system? Some researchers' findings point in this direction (see Robert Crutchfield, George S. Bridges and Susan R.Pitchford (1994:167).   Richey Mann, (1993:166) concluded from her review of the research literature on racial inequalities in the criminal justice that the inconclusiveness and disparities in findings are due largely to "scant concentration on portentous actions and decisions occurring earlier on the route to court after an arrest has been affected." An oversight she labeled misleading, since it has been found that "when racial differences in processing occur, they are likely to occur at stages prior to final sentencing."

These include preventive detention, and the assignment of bail at a financial level that denies minorities the opportunity to make bond. When bonds are set at high levels relative to a minority defendant's financial means, or those of their relatives, then they are unable to raise the amount, and must remain in detention until their case is heard. New York City has nearly 20,000 detainees who are 93% Black and Latino, and many of whom are in this situation.

Prosecutor's discretion may have detrimental effects on minorities at each step of the criminal justice process, ranging from charging grand jury indictments, to plea bargaining, and final court disposition. Poor and minority defendants are more likely to waive their constitutional right to trial and plea bargain in the hopes of obtaining more lenient sentences (Richey Mann, 1993:166). Prosecutors tend to overcharge minority defendants if the victim is white (p.204). The quality of criminal defense tends to be poorer for minorities in the criminal justice process, where they are overly dependent on public defenders. These attornies are often young, recent law school graduates, with little experience in criminal cases. These public defenders are sometimes too pliant with the judges and prosecutors, to their client's detriment.

The Triple Blows of Criminalization

1. The Negation of the Social Structure

There are at least three major impacts of Black and Latino male criminalization, social, economic and political, which have far reaching ramifications. Among the negative social impacts is a greatly reduced number of desirable Black and Latino males available to their women and children.   This means that there is an unavailability of men for companionship, economic support, marriage, procreation, and community leadership; and to serve as supporters, protectors and positive role models for children.

2. The Neutralization of Political Power

One of the major political impacts of criminalization is the negation of political empowerment.   When a person is convicted of a felony, their civil rights, including the right to register and vote, are automatically rescinded. This right can only be restored if the ex-offender's sentence has expired (persons on work release and parole are still not eligible to vote). That individual must take the initiative to apply for a "Certificate of Relief from Civil Disability" in order to have their voting rights reinstated. The courts and Board of Elections then make a determination. Then the ex-offender still must register and vote, in order to exercise their restored constitutional rights as a U.S. citizen.   There are thousands of ex-offenders in Black and Latino communities who, due to the above restrictions, do not have the right to vote, and as a result of their criminalization, a huge amount of electoral power in Black and Latino communities has been negated.

3. The Neutralization of Economic Power

The criminalization of Black and Latino males greatly damages their employability. Conviction for a

DBC

DuBois Bunche Center for Public Policy   MEDGAR EVERS COLLEGE, C.U.N.Y.

crime is automatic grounds for disqualification for many types of civil service, and private sector jobs. There is a high correlation between incarceration and lack of education. There is little education and almost no meaningful job training for inmates in prison. Thus ex-offenders seeking employment are likely not to have the requisite education, training and skills to enhance their employability in the job market. These factors constitute major liabilities in a highly competitive, white collar, service economy, along with a lack of jobs in local neighborhoods, particularly semi-skilled, basic manufacturing employment. There is also increasing job competition from immigrant populations in certain low wage job sectors. Thus, the prison experience of many adults in Black and Latino communities contributes in great measure, to the negation of economic empowerment in those communities.

IV. Racial Disparity in New York City's Judiciary[13]

The ultimate arbiter of the criminal justice system is the judiciary. Legislators legislate criminal laws, police apprehend law violators, and lawyers defend and prosecute alleged perpetrators. But it is the judges who decide the legality of the law; conduct the trials; determine the defendant's innocence or guilt, sometimes with the help of a jury whom they instruct and direct; and sentence the convicted.

This report rejects the notion that no white police officers, prosecutors, judges or wardens are capable of treating Black and Latino males in a fair and just manner. However this report does argue that the criminal justice system, like most other white controlled American institutions, is imbued with some levels of institutional racism, in which Black and Latino males do not always receive fair and just treatment by of this criminal justice system.   One of the tell-tale signs of institutional racism is the overwhelmingly white control of a system or institution, within which Blacks are required to operate and "be operated upon." Let us

---

[13] Reports : 1994 Annual Report, The Franklin H. Williams Judicial Commission On Minorities; N.Y.C. Office Of Court Administration and Unified Court System data; The New York Red Book, 1991-92, p.458.

briefly examine New York City's court administration and judiciary for some illustrations.

The New York City Court System is part of the statewide Unified Court System, with over 13,000 employees. The statewide workforce is 78% white; while senior officials and administrators are 92% white. New York City is 50% Black and Latino, but defendants in its criminal justice system are over 90% Black and Latino. Senior administrators in New York City's Civil Court are 88% white; in Family Court they are 80% white; and in Criminal Court they are 82% white. New York City's 19 County Clerk officials are all white.

The N.Y.S. Supreme Court has twelve judicial districts throughout the state; and four of these twelve districts cover New York City. The First District covers Manhattan, and their senior court officials are 71% white. The Second District covers Brooklyn and Staten Island, and their senior court officials are 78% white. The Eleventh District covers Queens, and their senior court officials are 80% white. The Twelfth District covers the Bronx, and their senior court officials are 83% white. Citywide, 30 out of 39, or 77% of state supreme court officials and administrators in New York City are white.

Criminal, Family & Civil Court Judges: Racial Composition

Now let's examine the judiciary itself. New York City Family Court, Criminal Court and non-elected Civil Court Judges are all appointed by the Mayor, upon screening and recommendation by key Bar associations. This process is controlled by prominent white attorneys and by the Mayor's Committee on the Judiciary. The Mayor's senior advisors, particularly if they are attorneys or jurists, can play an influential role in mayoral appointments to the judiciary. Former Mayor Dinkins appointed prominent African-American, Basil Paterson, Esq., as his Chair of the Mayor's Committee on the Judiciary. A significant proportion of Dinkins cabinet members were Black, Latino and female, including attorneys and jurists. During his tenure, Mayor Dinkins appointed the highest number and percentage of minorities and women to the Family, Criminal and Civil Court benches in New York City history.[14]

Mayor Giuliani has nearly an all-white mayoral cabinet, in a city that is 56% non-white. The sole non-white, Ninfa Segarra, is Puerto Rican. To date, Mayor Guliani's appointment of minorities to the judiciary is far less than the Dinkins record.

In 1994 the Family Court had 3 Black judges, 4 Latino judges and 38 white judges, or 84% white judges, for a court processing some 90% Black and Latino youth for the juvenile justice system. The Criminal Court had 7 Black judges, 3 Latino judges and 93 white judges, or 89% white judges processing some 90% Black and Latino adults for the criminal justice system. The Civil Court had 16 Black judges, 7 Latino judges, 2 Asian judges and 93 white judges, or 79% white judges. It should be noted that the vast majority of non-white civil court judges are elected out of local civil court districts

---

[14] Review of records of mayoral appointments to the judiciary.

covering predominantly Black and Latino neighborhoods, and their numbers are merged into the total.
Thus, the white percentage of appointed civil court
judges is much higher.

State Supreme Court Judges: Racial Composition

A racial analysis of New York State Supreme
Court and Court of Claims (drug court) judges sitting in
New York City is just as dismal, despite the fact that the
vast majority of supreme court judges are elected.
Elected supreme court judges must first be nominated at
a judicial district convention, which is dominated by the
county Democratic Party apparatus, which negotiates
racial, ethnic, political and geographic allocation of these
judgeships, with key political players within and outside
of the Democratic Party. Citywide, 243 of 296 supreme
court judges, or 82% are white.

The following is a borough by borough racial
analysis of supreme court judges. The Bronx has 5
Black, 4 Latino and 44 white judges, or 83% white.
Brooklyn has 13 Black, 5 Latino and 67 white judges, or
79% white. Manhattan has 12 Black, 4 Latino, and 80
white judges, or 83% white. Queens has 8 Black, 1
Latino, 1 Asian and 45 white judges, or 82% white.
Finally, all of Staten Island's 7 judges are white.
Brooklyn and Manhattan have 34 out of 52, or 65% of all
Black and Latino Supreme Court judges in New York
City.

It is not coincidental that these two boroughs
have African-American Democratic County leaders:

Assemblyman Clarence Norman, Jr. in Brooklyn; and
Assemblyman Herman Farrell, Jr. in Manhattan who
likely used their political leverage to achieve these
results. These results notwithstanding, there is a lawsuit
by the Center for Constitutional Rights et. al., entitled
France v. Cuomo, which is presently making its way
through the U.S. Justice Dept. and the courts. This lawsuit alleges among other things, that there is a pattern of
racial discrimination with respect to electing, nominating
and selecting New York judges.

White Judges - Black & Latino Defendants

Overall, there are approximately 325 judges who
preside over the criminal justice system in New York
City: 274 of these judges, or 84% are white.   In the
N.Y.S. Supreme Court, Criminal Part, 143 of the 176
judges serving are white (81%).   In N.Y.C. Criminal
Court 93 of the 104 judges serving are white (89%).   In
N.Y.C. Family Court 38 of the 45 judges which impact
the juvenile justice system are white (84%).   In summary, one might subtitle the New York City criminal justice
system, "White Judges - Black and Latino Defendants."

Perception is reality, and many in the Black and
Latino community perceive that justice is not fair,
impartial and color blind, as the textbooks, civics lessons
and constitutions portray justice to be.   In New York's
criminal justice system, the judges, prosecutors, police
and prison guards are overwhelmingly white; and the
indictees, defendants, convicts and ex-offenders are
overwhelmingly Black and Latino.   There is a standard
notion in minority communities that "justice" means

"just us."   In other words, the meting out of punishment for crimes is perceived as being for Blacks and Latinos only.   Conversely, corrupt and brutal white police officers, wealthy white collar criminals, corporate welfare cheats, and white organized crime figures seem to routinely avoid punishment for their crimes.

One of the key factors which would alter their perception of justice as one-sided, would be for Blacks and Latinos to see themselves represented on both sides of the bar, and not just on the receiving end of justice. In keeping with this nation's democratic theory of representative institutions, the solution demands that there be more Black and Latino judges, prosecutors and police officers, who are more reflective of New York City's culturally and racially diverse communities, on whose behalf justice is administered. Black and Latino youth should receive an early legal education on the critical importance of avoiding encounters with the criminal justice system. Minority males, in particular, must be protected by family and community from becoming system statistics.   These negative encounters limit their life opportunities, disqualify them from future law enforcement and other careers, and neutralize them politically, economically and socially.

V. The Political Economy of the Prison Industrial Complex

The criminal justice system is not just an institutional mechanism to provide justice, it is also a business, a criminal justice enterprise, a prison industrial complex. This industry has created thousands of jobs in scores of occupations, such as clerical, data processing, janitorial, police, prison guards, court officers, paralegals, lawyers, and judges. At the entrepreneurial level, the construction industry, Wall St. bond financiers, corporate attorneys, and myriad contractual services and suppliers, have benefited from the multi-billion dollar business of financing, building, renovating and expanding jails and prisons (Richey Mann, 1993:127-128; Ellis, 1992)

The medium of exchange, the commodity of this massive industry are Black and Latino males from Central Brooklyn and a few similar communities. A major component of this industrial complex is the multi-billion economy in goods, services, and contracts flowing through upstate prison facilities which are the backbone of several upstate local economies where most Republican legislators reside.

There are well over 100,000 jobs in the prison industrial complex, which are linked to the criminalization, apprehension, detention, trial, conviction, incarceration and supervision of young Black and Latino males. To mention just some of the key employment compo-

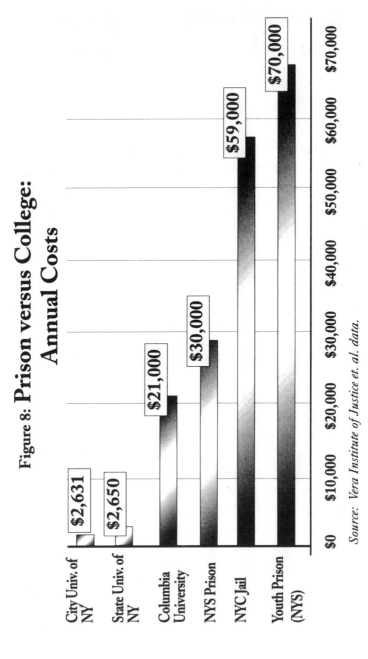

Figure 8: Prison versus College: Annual Costs

City Univ. of NY	$2,631
State Univ. of NY	$2,650
Columbia University	$21,000
NYS Prison	$30,000
NYC Jail	$59,000
Youth Prison (NYS)	$70,000

Source: Vera Institute of Justice et. al. data.

nents: New York City has 50,000 police and corrections personnel and 3,500 District Attorney personnel. New York State has 40,000 corrections, police, probation and parole personnel. The state court system has 3,500 judges and 12,000 court personnel; and much of the state apparatus is concentrated in New York City.

In his article, "Trading Textbooks for Prison Cells," (1991), criminologist William Chamblis demonstrated how significantly public expenditures on criminal justice have risen over the past 20 years, so that the expenditure on law enforcement far exceeds that on education. The federal government increased its spending on criminal justice by 29 percent, much of that increase going to " the war on drugs."

Chambliss argued that America has grown so dependent upon a single approach to the problem of crime, that allocations to criminal justice are rarely debated. New York City, faced with a deficit of $2 billion in 1991, contemplated spending $375 million to add 1,000 beds to the jail system; and spending $66 million per year to hire 1,058 patrol officers. He cited Department of Justice figures (1988) which show nationally states' spending on police and corrections, going from $8 billion in 1969, to $80 billion in 1989; and spending on prison construction, maintenance and parole nearly doubling in the last ten years (pp. 4-5).

He maintains that the expenditures continue to rise despite "the near total failure of the criminal justice system." He cited the issue of recidivism, where a National Institute of Justice study estimated that there was a 62.5 % re-arrest rate of 108,580 persons released from prisons in 11 states, within three years of release. He argued that this pattern is consistent with research dating back to the 19th century. Yet in 1991, states laid off teachers and cut social services while the criminal justice system not only remained virtually immune from cuts, but was in fact expanded. (Chambliss, 1991, p.8).

$5 Billion Industry and 80,000 Jobs

The Vera Institute of Justice, using figures from the New York City Office of Management and Budget, calculated the annual costs of the criminal justice system for New York City, in FY 1994, at close to $2.5 billion. The annual operating budget of the key state criminal justice agencies, of corrections, probation, parole, police and courts is easily another $2.5 billion. Thus the annual operating budget alone for the city and state apparatus is at least $5 billion a year. This does not include additional annual capital expenditures in the hundreds of millions for court and prison construction[15].

The fear of crime, which has driven criminal justice expenditures, has several sources. First and foremost is the incidence of homicide, the ultimate representation of the horrors of crime. In 1992, there were 1,995 reported homicides in New York City. In 1993 there were 1,946 homicides; and in 1994 there were 1,561 homicides in New York City. Thus in a three-year period, from 1992 to 1994, homicides dropped by 434 murders, or 22%. This was due in perhaps significant measure, to the "Safe Streets - Safe City" anti-crime pro-

---

[15] "Narrative Summary...SFY 1995," Ways and Means Committee, op.cit.

gram, which Mayor Dinkins inaugurated during his tenure, in partnership with the City Council and state legislature. This program was engineered by Dinkins' Police Commissioner Lee Brown, and added thousands of more police on street patrol.

Nonetheless, there persists the sensational media coverage of crime, which pumps up the fear of crime because it sells newspapers. The "fear factor" then creates the climate to justify accelerated spending on the criminal justice system. Some law enforcement officials and personnel, along with their union and professional organizations play a significant role in stirring up the fear of crime, or capitalizing on public empathy with their law enforcement role. These special interests use powerful lobbying to pressure vulnerable politicians to allocate more power and resources to their domain in the name of "fighting the criminals," when their real agenda is as much about bureaucratic turf and self-aggrandizement.

Privatizing Prisons?

The business section of *The New York Times*, August 14, 1994 (p.3) carried the headline,"Privatizing American Prisons Slowly." The article reports that 13 states currently allow private prisons and approximately 2% of the nation's inmates are housed in such facilities. Corrections Corporation of America is the leader in this $250 million growing industry. The company is headquartered in Nashville and owns 23 prisons under contract in seven states which service one-third of all prisoners in private prisons. This company made 57% profit

DBC

DuBois Bunche Center for Public Policy   MEDGAR EVERS COLLEGE, C.U.N.Y.

in 1993 and 30% in the first half of 1994. Over the next two years, it is expected that the company's 13,000 beds will increase by 85% and profits will more than double.

Among major critics of private prisons are correction officer unions and civil liberties advocates. Privatized prisons offering non-unionized, non-pension employment, is a major concern of civil service correction guards. Prisoner abuse scandals, which is a concern of advocates, led to the discontinuation of private prisons in an earlier era. According to the *Times* article, private prisons are experimenting with programs to give prisoners marketable skills. At one facility the Corrections Corporation is putting in a garment factory to make disposable hazardous waste suits. Thus, there is the danger of prison labor becoming cheap labor which undercuts the broader labor market.

Along these very lines, Richey Mann (1993:128) observed:

> "Nor can we overlook the enhanced capitalistic (ruling class) opportunities: the construction industry that builds the jails and prisons; private entrepreneurs who benefit from cheap (slave) labor in the production of their products through prison industries; and the profiteers who function as suppliers to this multi-billion dollar business. The criminalization of minority peoples supplies the human fuel to maintain this constantly expanding enterprise."

Mann (1993:221) went on further to say that:

> "The mass of Americans is deceived by the law and order ideology for it promises that one can achieve "peace of mind" and the "good life" without addressing such underlying issues as poverty, racial conflict,

education, health care, population pressures, and the allocation of resources."

In earlier times, Republican Presidents Nixon and Reagan pushed a "law and order" national policy agenda. Today, with their "Contract With America" anti-crime legislation, the Republican-controlled 104th Congress is pushing a 1990s version of the law and order agenda, which is being mirrored at state and local levels throughout the nation. Starting with Nixon's election in 1968, every president and most other politicians seeking office have parlayed law and order, and being tough on crime, into winning elections.

The incumbent president, Bill Clinton, promised tough measures against crime, and succeeded in 1994 with the Omnibus Crime Control Act, a $30 billion package to hire more cops, build more prisons, ban assault weapons and provide crime prevention resources. Now the Republicans have labeled as "pork" -- the provisions for the social programs to help keep youngsters out of the criminal justice system, and they are now in the process of gutting these provisions, and further toughening national crime legislation, under their "Taking Back Our Streets" package of bills which is discussed in further detail, in a subsequent section of this report.

According to the Correctional Association of New York, it costs $30,000 to maintain one prisoner in a New York State prison for one year and $59,000 in a New York City jail for the same period of time. The comparable expenditure for one year of college at C.U.N.Y. or S.U.N.Y. is $2,700. (See Figure 8.) Prison construction

DBC

DuBois Bunche Center for Public Policy   MEDGAR EVERS COLLEGE, C.U.N.Y.

has also accelerated to accommodate the rapid growth of prisoners. Since 1983, Governor Cuomo built 29,000 new prison spaces at overall costs of $5 billion and an annual maintenance cost of $870 million. This extensive prison construction exceeded the number built by all previous administrations. These new spaces are being used primarily for drug offenders, a category that has grown from 11 percent of commitments in 1980 to 44 percent in 1993. The rate of imprisonment for violent crimes, in the meantime, has declined from 63% of commitments in 1983 to 35 % in 1993. According to the Correctional Association of New York, the City's operational budget for jails grew from $120 million in 1981 to about $765 million for 1991, a 500% increase. Eddie Ellis (1990), a criminal justice researcher and system graduate, has observed in his work that prison construction, the location of prisons, the escalating rate of Black/Latino incarceration, and the high rate of recidivism among parolees are interrelated phenomena, forming an economic system of support for upstate white communities.

VI. Federal and State Crime Legislation:

More Laws, More Inmates, More Prisons

There is a pronounced trend in recent years, towards more stringent crime legislation at the federal and state levels, and this process has accelerated, with the Republican takeover of the 104th Congress. This section discusses a number of significant pieces of crime legislation at the federal government and New York State levels, which are likely to have major impacts on Black and Latino communities, if implemented.

Federal Legislation

In September 1994, President Bill Clinton signed into law, The Violent Crime Control and Law Enforcement Act of 1994, (Public Law 103-322), also known as the Omnibus Crime Control Act, which had been passed by the Democratically controlled 103rd Congress. In the November 1994 elections, the Republican Party gained control of the national legislature in the House and the Senate, and introduced a radically more severe crime legislative package, with the goal of repealing many of the provisions of the Omnibus Crime Control Act, and supplanting it with major crime legislative proposals which are part of their "Contract With America." This section will discuss the 1994 Omnibus Crime Control Act, followed by the major

Contract With America crime legislation, a package of six bills, collectively known as the "Taking Back Our Streets Act of 1995."

The Omnibus Crime Control Act of 1994 [16]

This legislation is a $ 30 billion package providing:

- $ 8.8 billion to hire 100,000 more police officers;
- $ 7.9 billion to build more prisons;
- $ 4.1 billion for crime prevention programs, including $ 377 million in block grants;
- $ 3 billion to help federal and state officials deal with criminal and illegal aliens;
- $ 2.6 billion additional funding for the FBI, DEA, INS, other Justice and Treasury Dept. units and U.S. Attorneys, to deal with violent criminals;
- $ 1 billion for domestic violence programs; and
- $ 1 billion for drug courts; and $ 383 million for prison drug treatment;

Some major provisions of the 1994 Omnibus Crime Act include:

- a ban on the manufacture of certain assault weapons and ammunition;
- expanding the death penalty to cover 60 additional offenses;
- strengthening federal licensing for firearms dealers;
- defining new insurance and telemarketing fraud crimes;

---

[16] Memorandum From The U.S. Attorney General. Sept. 15, 1994. Wash. D.C.

- providing new and stiffer penalties for crimes by gang members;
- authorizing adult prosecution for 13-year-olds for certain serious crimes;
- stiffer penalties for sex offenders;
- "three strikes" mandatory life imprisonment without parole for three or more serious felonies;
- federal grant programs for states and localities for community policing and other crime prevention initiatives; and
- establishment of the President's Crime Prevention Council.

" Contract With America:
Taking Back Our Streets Legislation "[17]

As part of their implementation of the "Contract With America," the Republican controlled U.S. House of Representatives under the leadership of Speaker Newt Gingrich, has passed several crime bills, including:

- **H.R. 665 - The Victim Restitution Act Of 1995**

Mandates that persons convicted of violent or white collar crime be required to pay victim and other persons claiming harm, full restitution for damages. Payment could be set without regard to felon's ability to pay, and

---

[17] Sources: Congressional Research Service, Library Of Congress via Internet (www:thomas.loc.gov) 5-6/95; "Embryonic Signs Of The Police State: The Implications of Six GOP Crime Bills On Blacks, Working Class and Most Americans." Crim. Justice Research Backgrounder #3, Congr'l Black Caucus Fndn. 3/7/95; Democratic Study Group Fact Sheet No.103-45, 11/28/94.

would be a condition of probation, parole or release. Failure to pay could result in reincarceration or selling of felon's property.

• **H.R. 666 - Exclusionary Rule Reform Act of 1995**

The Fourth Amendment to the U.S. Constitution guarantees every citizen freedom from unreasonable search and seizure by the government. The exclusionary rule is established by U.S. Supreme Court decisions which require judges to exclude evidence obtained in violation of the Fourth Amendment. In most cases police are required to obtain a search warrant from a judge, before they can search and seize a person's property, and use it as evidence in a trial. This bill allows the police to make "warrantless" searches and seizures when acting in "good faith."

• **H.R. 667 - Violent Criminal Incarceration Act of 1995**

The 1994 Omnibus Crime Control Act allocated $ 7.9 billion for prison construction. This bill increases amounts to $ 10.5 billion. Half of this money would only go to states who can document increased numbers of violent felons since 1993, whose sentences are longer and serve more time before release. The other 50% or $ 5.2 billion is for "truth in sentencing" grants for states where violent felons serve at least 85% of their sentences. This sharply limits a state's discretion; and according to the Justice Dept., 47 states and the District of Columbia would have to change their laws to be in conformity with these criteria. This bill also makes it easier to dismiss legal complaints by prisoners.

• H.R. 668 - Criminal Alien Deportation Improvements Act Of 1995

Like the 1994 Omnibus Act, this authorizes federal judges to enter deportation orders at sentencing, eliminating the need for separate deportation hearings. It authorizes the INS to begin deportation proceedings when an alien is sentenced to five years in prison. It authorizes the Justice Dept. to issue a deportation order without a hearing, for aliens convicted of certain felonies. About $ 650 million a year from the prison construction fund, would be allocated to reimburse states for the costs of incarcerating illegal aliens.

• H.R. 728 - Local Government Law Enforcement Block Grants Act Of 1995

This bill eliminates $ 5.5 billion from the 1994 Omnibus Crime Control Act for items including: community crime prevention intitatives; drug treatment programs; intensive supervision for non-violent felony offenders; school and summer youth programs; midnight basketball; ounce of prevention grants; and it eliminates $ 1.3 billion to hire and train 20,000 police officers a year for five years. This bill establishes a new block grant program, with greatly reduced funding for crime prevention activities.

• H.R. 729 - The Effective Death Penalty Act of 1995

Under the 1994 Omnibus Crime Act, a jury would have to consider mitigating circumstances in determining whether to impose the death penalty, life imprisonment without parole, or a lesser sentence. This bill greatly reduces the jury's discretion and eliminates life imprisonment without parole as as an option for federal death penalty crimes. This bill reduces the timeframe and the number of appeals for a death row inmate (writ of habeas corpus); and makes it easier to impose and carry out the death penalty.

The prognosis for this "Contract With America" federal crime legislation is that if it becomes law, even more Black and Latino males, than the present disproportionate numbers, will be incarcerated, for longer periods of time. More Black and Latino inmates will receive the death penalty, a punishment which has proven to be racially discriminatory in its application, and not a deterrent to violent crimes.[18]   Black and Latino incarceration is not just at crisis levels in New York, but it is a national crisis in Black and Latino communities throughout this nation, which will be further accelerated if the proposed federal crime legislation of the 104th Congress is implemented.

Much of this federal crime legislation is also being mirrored at the state and local levels, as we shall see when we review some of New York State's recent

---

[18] See, "The Death Penalty," Briefing Paper No.8, American Civil Liberties Union. 1994.

crime legislation. In fact, in some cases, the federal legislation mandates state and local conformity, in order to receive federal funding. This approach flatly contradicts other major "Contract With America" legislative initiatives known as "mandate relief" and regulatory reform. For example, in the case of eligibility for federal prison construction funding, state and local prison sentencing policies must first conform to strict quotas spelled out in the proposed federal "Truth In Sentencing" requirements.

Blacks in State Prisons

In 22 states with Black Congressional representation, Black prisoners as a percentage of total state prison population, range from 35% in Oklahoma and California; to 98% in Washington D.C.[19] :

- Over 70% Black prisoner population: Wash.D.C., Louisiana, Maryland, Mississippi;

- 60 - 69% Black prisoner population: Alabama, Georgia, Illinois, New Jersey, South Carolina, Virginia;

- 50 - 59% Black prisoner population: Florida, *New York*, Ohio, Pennsylvania;

- 40- 49% Black prisoner population: Missouri, Tennessee, Texas.

---

[19] Table 1: Selected Crime-Related Statistics Of States With African American Members Of Congress, in "The Implications Of Six GOP Crime Bills" CBC policy paper.

New York State Crime Legislation

The following is a summary of selected crime legislation passed by the Republican controlled, politically conservative New York State Senate during the 1994 and 1995 legislative sessions. [20]

1994 Legislative Session

S.3385, 6338-A, 6309-C - "Three Strikes" Legislation[21]

Three bills passed the Senate, which would impose mandatory life imprisonment for certain habitual felony offenders.

S.546 -   Prosecutor's Appeal of Lenient Sentences

This bill passed the Senate, and allows a prosecutor in a criminal case to appeal a sentence as too lenient,

S.919 -   Resisting Arrest -- A Felony

This bill passed the Senate and makes more serious a crime, and imposes a greater penalty for the crime of resisting arrest and using force against a police officer.

---

[20] Source: Internet, Senate.State.NY.US, Marcia White and Tara Ellis, "New York State Senate Reports - Weekly Legislative Highlights." 1994-95.
[21] For a major critique of 'Three Strikes Legislation,' see "10 Reasons To Oppose '3 Strikes You're Out,'" An American Civil Liberties Union Briefer. 1994.

S.1156 - Probationer's Payment Fees

This bill passed the Senate, and requires a probationer to reimburse New York City or County probation offices for probation services as a condition of probation or discharge.

S.1898 - Parole Release and Deportation

Under certain conditions, this bill permits the Parole Board to notify the relevant district attorney, and grant early release of an inmate who is subject to deportation by the INS.

S.5321 - Prisoners to pay their Jail Expenses

This bill passed the Senate, and requires non-indigent inmates to reimburse the local jail for food, medical and other maintenance expenses. And female inmates who have children in jail will pay child care costs. Once an inmate is released, willful violation of the reimbursement agreement can result in up to six months imprisonment or garnishment of income. Individuals can apply for a waiver.

S.6378 - Exoneration of Police Officers

This bill passed the Senate, and exonerates police and other peace officers from tort liability for damages based on personal injury to the plaintiff, where officer shows evidence that plaintiff's injury occured while officer was attempting to effect an arrest, and other conditions.

1995 Legislative Session

New York State Budget, FY 96 and 97: Massive Build-up of Prison Cells

The state capital budget passed in June 1995, authorized $120 million bonding authority for the N.Y.S. Urban Development Corporation (UDC), to buy two upstate correctional facilities from New York City, Riverview and Cape Vincent. This will expand state prison capacity.

Note: The Governor's Proposed Budget for FY 1996-97, released in December 1995, requested $476 million for three more maximum security prisons upstate and 8,800 more prison cells; and proposes to transfer 16-18 year olds to adult prisons.

Elimination of College Tuition Assistance (TAP) for Prison Inmates. Aid to Localities Budget, FY 96.

A.7881 Increased Sentencing for Violent Offenders

Expands crimes requiring mandatory state prison terms; increases mandatory minimum and maximum sentences; eliminates parole; drastically decreases "time off for good behaviour" credit; eliminates indeterminate sentencing with judicial discretion and replaces it with determinate sentencing with no judicial discretion[22]

---

[22] See "Revised and Updated Memorandum ConcerningA.7881," N.Y.S. Defenders Assoc., Inc. 5/31/95.

DBC

DuBois Bunche Center for Public Policy   MEDGAR EVERS COLLEGE, C.U.N.Y.

S.5281 / A.7991 -   Longer Prison Sentences

Increases jail terms for violent felons and creates a Sentencing Commission to study this legislation and report back to the Governor and the Legislature. It promotes drug treatment for non-violent felons and parole violators; and expedites deportation of non-violent illegal aliens.

S.4381-A -   Easier Drug Convictions

In certain cases, eliminates the requirement that the prosecutor must prove that the defendant knew the weight of a controlled substance or marihuana in possession or for sale, making it easier to obtain a conviction.

S.4408 -   Tougher Standards for Prisoner Lawsuits

Imposes filing fees on prisoners who bring litigation; and imposes prisoner sanctions for legal actions determined by a judge to be frivolous or without merit.

S.3561 -   Expanded PINS Status
(More youth criminalized)

Expands definition of "Persons In Need of Supervision" to include any minor required to attend school. Increases enforcement of compulsory education laws.

S.2597 -   Youthful Offender Restitution

Gives Family Court more power to impose restitution and community service sanctions on youth.

DBC
DuBois Bunche Center for Public Policy   **MEDGAR EVERS COLLEGE, C.U.N.Y.**

S.2587 -   Parent Liability for Child Offenses

Makes parents liable for malicious acts of their children
10-18 years old. The bill also permits recovery from parents of court costs, legal fees and other expenses.

S.2595 -   More Criminal Background Checks

Requires criminal background check for any applicant
seeking a license or registration as a child care provider
in New York State.   S.1984-A would prohibit the hiring
of any person as Division For Youth Aide if they were
ever convicted of a felony.

S.539 -   Tracking Student Criminal Activity

Requires full reimbursement of state assisted financial
aid, by any student engaging in criminal activities that
yield unreported income. The Division of Criminal
Justice Services will collaborate with the Higher
Education Services Corp. to catch perpetrators.

S.2614 -   DFY Escape Alarms

Requires an escape alarm on all Division For Youth
secure facilities, which is audible for a two mile radius.
DFY is also required to notify local authorities, residents
and media within fifteen minutes of discovery of any
DFY resident's unauthorized absence.

S.3065 -   Juvenile Offender Status Expanded

Makes 12-15 year olds eligible for juvenile offender status if accused of burglarizing a home.

S.5197 -   Prosecution of Juvenile Escapees

Makes it illegal for a person under 16 years old to escape a detention facility if placed there by a Family Court; and provides that such person will be prosecuted as a juvenile delinquent.

S.2612 -   Drug Sales in Housing Projects

Increases penalties for drug sales in and around housing projects (Similar to harsher penalties for drug sales in and around schools, which bill already passed the Legislature.)

S.2256 -   Drugs / Revocation of Driver's License

Extends for another year, state law requiring revocation of a driver's license upon a third conviction for certain drug related offenses. This legislation continues New York's eligibility for federal highway money.

S.670 - Felony for Transporting Illegal Immigrants

Makes a person guilty of a felony for transporting illegal immigrants into New York; and the bill allows for seizure or forfeiture of property used to transport illegal aliens.

S.1296 -   Reorganizing the Judiciary

Reorganizes the downstate judicial departments, to more efficiently handle court caseloads. Brooklyn, Queens and the Bronx would be affected in New York City.

S.3234 -   Firearms -- Increased Penalties

Increases penalties for illegal possession of a firearm, for anyone convicted of a felony in the last ten years.

S.4068 -   Assaulting a Police Officer

Adds aggravated assault on a police officer as a violent felony offense.

S.4588 -   Easier to Obtain a Pistol Permit

Removes requirement that a pistol permit applicant should demonstrate proper need for a pistol.

S.3919 -   Longer Sentencing

For persistent violent felons, raises mandatory minimum from 2 to 10 years; and raises the maximum from 25 years to life.

S.2352 -   Drug Free Parks

Makes it a felony to sell drugs in or near parks or playgrounds.

S.4140 -   Weapons in Schools

Requires a minimum one-year suspension for students who bring weapons to school.

S.3089-A - Reporting Illegal Immigrant Students

Requires all higher education institutions to verify immigration status of their students, and expel illegal enrollees.

S.3091 - Reporting Illegal Alien Arrestees

Requires police to notify INS of any arrestee suspected of being an illegal alien.

S.2826-A Financial Penalties for Censured Attorneys

Requires any attorney censured, suspended or removed due to misconduct, to pay the costs of investigation and disciplinary proceedings.

S.1410 - School Violence -- Felony Crime

Makes assault on a school employee a felony.

S.3494 - Fingerprinting Minor Felons

Requires fingerprinting of all minors accused of committing a felony; and other provisions.

S.520 - Police Tracking Truants

Requires school official to turn over to police, identity of any child with five days unexcused absence.

S.2872 -   Offensive Behaviour -- A Crime

Makes aggressive begging a crime; prohibits sitting or lying on commercial sidewalks during specified times.

S.449-A   No Police Liability for Deadly Force

Protects police from liability for use of deadly force against criminals.

S.692   Three Strikes and You're Out

Mandatory life imprisonment for third serious felony.

S.187   Unlimited Consecutive Sentencing

Removes current limits on total sentencing to allow consecutive sentencing for each crime.

S.2850 -   New and Improved Death Penalty

Restored death penalty in New York when South Africa's Supreme Court abolished its death penalty.

S.197 -   Resisting Arrest -- A Felony

Raises crime from Misdemeanor to Class E Felony.

PBA Legislation [23] -

A June 1995 New York Times Editorial entitled

---

[23] "To Albany: Don't Undermine the N.Y.P.D.," Editorial page, A20. New York Times, June 29,1995.

"To Albany: Don't Undermine the N.Y.P.D.," discussed a package of 4 bills in Albany, sponsored by the Patrolmen's Benevolent Association, the police officer's union. *The Times* reported:

"(One bill would)...strip the Police Commissioner of final authority to terminate or suspend officers who flout department policy.

Suspensions and dismissals would become subject to mandatory (outside) arbitration. ...Other bills would unjustly raise the incomes of many officers...(and) require mandatory raises... for certain job categories... regardless of whether the raises were warranted by performance. A related bill would legislate the number of detectives that the city would have to maintain in each rank...guaranteeing...the highest pay levels.

Yet another bill would sabotage the merger of the city's three police forces. The Legislature's tampering with the merger could cost the city millions in federal subsidies..."

Conclusion

It should be clear from the foregoing legislative review, that some major aspects of the reality of "crime" are not objective, but subjective and politically driven. A major part of the question of who and what is criminal, is based on who legislates and therefore, defines the "criminal" and "criminality." One can criminalize an individual or a whole group of people, simply by expropriating the power to define what constitutes legality and illegality, and therefore who is a criminal in society. Black people in America, through their experience of institutionalized slavery, subjugation and control, have been the objects and subjects of this pheomenon of criminalization, for over 300 years.

In his great work, *In The Matter Of Color*, Judge A. Leon Higginbotham, Jr. identified perhaps the first statute of Black criminalization in the history of this country. The Slave Codes Of 1680-82 of the Commonwealth of Virginia made it a crime for Black slaves to: gather in large numbers (freedom of assembly); carry any type of weapons (right to bear arms); leave their plantations without a certificate from their master (freedom of movement); or lift their hand to a white person (right to self-defense). Violation of this statute was punishable by severe whipping; and resisting lawful apprehension was punishable by death [24].

Some of the noted criminal justice legislation has positive applications, in controlling crime and punishing

---

[24] A. Leon Higginbotham,Jr., "Part II, The Black Experience In Colonial America." pp.38-40. *In The Matter Of Color, Race & The American Legal Process: The Colonial Period.*

criminals, for no crime should go unpunished. However, many aspects of this legislation, while perhaps not having the intent, will nonetheless have the probable effect of disproportionately further criminalizing, incarcerating and executing Black and Latino males.

VII. Policy Recomendations and Conclusions

The criminal justice system, over the past 30 years, has successfully arrested, prosecuted, and imprisoned Blacks and Latinos in numbers that far exceed their representation in the population. The statistics and media reports and visual representations of criminals and criminality strongly implicate Blacks and Latinos almost to the exclusion of other racial and ethnic categories. In addition, there has been a tendency to impute Black racial status to a psychological predisposition to crime. Thus, Blacks who commit crimes are equated with animals, unrestrained, uncaring, and anti-social. The punishment is implied in the depiction--society must not tolerate "those animals." They need to be locked up, in much the same way that wild animals are caged. With public officials, media, and other sources constantly reiterating the need to "get tough" on crime, the general public has come to believe that crime is the number one problem in the nation and are willing to pay so that they can feel safe. How can this process of animalization and criminalization be refuted and reversed?

The criminalization of Blacks and Latinos is based largely on making the possession of relatively small quantities of drugs, a criminal offense. What are the options for decriminalizing? The Pataki administration and the state legislature recently modified the Rockefeller Drug Laws of 1973, to free up non-violent drug offenders from the prison system, in order to make more room for violent felony offenders. The same rigorous law enforcement should apply equally to offenders of all racial and ethnic backgrounds.

Major law enforcement resources should be directed to prevent the importation of drugs and guns into Black and Latino communities. Nationwide, the number of incarcerated Black males in prisons and jails, 1992-93 exceeds the number enrolled in higher education --583,00 to 537,00 (Mauer, 1994:18). The problem, however, extends beyond the difference of numbers in prisons or in college. The majority of those incarcerated have not even graduated from high school.

Education has not been a positive force in either developing or transforming Black and Latino youths in inner city communities from which the majority of the prison populations are drawn. Economic opportunities that help to develop understanding of the world of work, develop job skills, and earn income in legitimate ways, have practically disappeared from minority communities.

The low level of educational achievement impacts negatively upon job opportunities. This, in turn, stymies the ability to move into the social mainstream and become productive citizens. Education and training are prerequisites for responsible adulthood, especially for young men. Any resolution of crime in inner city communities must deal with the problematic issues of education, poverty and jobs. No responsible person makes the argument that crime should be excused on the basis of a person's poverty status. Nevertheless, a strong correlation exists between incarceration and poverty status. Elliot (1994:5) made the point that:

> "...race and class differences in serious violent offending are small during adolescence, but become substantial during the early adult years. This difference does not appear to be the result of differences in predispositions to violence, but in the continuity of violence once initiated. Race, in particular, is related to finding and holding a job, marriage and stable cohabiting rates. In essence, race and poverty are related to successfully making the transition   out of adolescence and into adult roles."

Major changes to the criminal justice system require a parallel focus on the other institutional arenas that are impacting negatively upon Black and Latino youth. One correction official at the Rikers Island facility in New York City summarized the condition and outlook of the youth she encountered there (PBS Interview with Charlayne Hunter Gault, April 11, 1991; and Assistant Commissioner Jane Jefers):

> --Lack of connection -- alienation and hopelessness;--no perception of opportunities;--no investment in the future --family, home, fathering of children;--immediate gratification --quick money from the drug trade;--viciousness and lack of remorse (they boast about their crimes);--belief that they will not be apprehended -- false sense of invincibility; --no expectation of living beyond twenty-five years of age: none of their friends do.

Dr. Mercer Sullivan, a socio-cultural anthropologist who did comparative research on young inner-city males in three neighborhoods - Black, Puerto Rican and White - in the early 1980s testified before the Select

Committee on Children, Youth, and Families, U.S.
House of Representatives, (July 25,1989:106-109) that:

> "... the crime careers of youths in all three
> neighborhoods started off very similarly and diverged
> over time as these youths confronted very basic dif-
> ferences in economic opportunity as well as differ-
> ences in local-level social control.

> Both white and minority youths we studied
> engaged in acts of non-violent theft and in extensive
> and sometimes deadly street-fighting while in their
> early and mid-teens. As they grew older, however,
> many of the minority youths became more heavily
> involved in crime as a source of fairly regular income.
> Their crimes grew increasingly systematic and violent
> as they passed from their middle to their late
> teens.(p108)

> Not only did these white youths have better
> access to employment than their minority peers, they
> also encountered stricter local-level social control.
> Local adults either retaliated themselves directly, or
> called the police. Their close relationship with the
> local police precinct was often based on ties between
> family and neighbors, since a number of police officers
> lived in the neighborhood.(p109)"

Sullivan further argued that the characteristics of
the communities in which people grow up provides the
means for assessing behavior and validly understanding
the behavioral choices individuals make. Like others, he
cites poverty, female-headed households and the
absence of men as role models for young males; and the
inability of the minority community to provide legitimate economic options to crime.

Marc Mauer (1994:19) reiterated similar findings claiming that:

> "While incarceration may be necessary to respond to certain violent behaviors, its role in enabling young offenders to make the transition to work and family is virtually nonexistent. For middle class youth who have access to resources, the transition is far more likely to take place successfully without any intervention by the criminal justice system."

If, as both Sullivan (1989) and Mauer (1994) concluded, youth can be effectively diverted from violent behaviors when they are provided with alternatives, then we must conclude that Black and Latino youths have not been provided with enough alternatives. In fact, very early on, they are exposed to the options of arrest, summons, or youthful offender status. This starts their encounter with the criminal justice system which effectively undermines other essential activities such as completing school and entering the labor force.

What must be done? The problem is societally and individually centered, and must be approached from those perspectives. At the community level, responsible individuals such as parents, older siblings, relatives and community support persons must take the initiative to teach young people the proper values and to take responsiblity for their actions. Strategies must also be developed: 1) to intervene and encourage law enforcement personnel to use minimum rather than maximum necessary options to redirect youth engaging in anti-social behaviour; and 2) to prevent law enforcement from behaving in ways inimical to the community's interests.

DBC
DuBois Bunche Center for Public Policy   MEDGAR EVERS COLLEGE, C.U.N.Y.

Elected and other public service officials, community organizations, and individuals must create pressure groups to redirect or help eliminate law enforcement practices that are discriminatory against minority youth and adults. A proactive approach as opposed to a reactive approach could help eliminate some of the negative statistics. For example, when a youth is arrested, an organized group making telephone calls to strategic persons or going to the precinct, may prevent a youngster from being branded and shunted into the criminal justice process. Research has shown that for some of the same crimes for which minority youth are being criminalized in their communities, white youth are being intercepted and diverted from the criminal justice system in their communities, by a sympathetic police officer, local priest, community leader or politician.

Crime prevention must not be left solely to the police, who have a limited role in preventing crime. Block by block, individuals must work in conjunction with law enforcement even as they demand that officers maintain professional standards in doing their work. The criminal justice system has limited effectiveness in preventing crime, and takes on the role of punishing, not rehabilitating criminals. Obvious sources of crime must be attacked. Drugs and guns do not originate in minority communities, yet these are major causes of crime, especially violent crime.

This report is an effort to discuss some of the salient issues which must be seriously addressed in order to resolve the critical and interlocking problems of race, crime and justice, particularly from the perspective of communities of color.

In closing, what follows are specific policy and programmatic recommendations which address several aspects of the problems of race, crime and justice. in most cases, these rationales are fairly obvious, and have already been discussed in previous segments of this report. A number of these recommendations are not dramatic new revelations, but are tried and effective solutions which are being negated in the present policy climate.

Policy and Programmatic Recommendations

• Establish a City Residency Requirement for NYC Police and other law enforcement personnel.

• The Police Department should hire more Blacks and Latinos as patrol officers; and promote more of them as mid-level and senior police officials.

• The Police Commissioner should take swift disciplinary action against all police officers who violate government laws and regulations.

• Increase security measures for Local Businesses in Black and Latino neighborhoods.

• Fund more Crime Prevention programs in Black and Latino neighborhoods.

• Promote domestic disarmament using toys for guns and other community amnesty programs. Use the full weight of government to stop the importation, sale and use of guns and drugs in minority communities.

• Fund more Youth Development programs in Black and Latino neighborhoods; generate more youth training and jobs, year-round.

• Ban sale of violent and offensive music to minors; stop the illegal sale of alcohol and tobacco products to minors.

• Organize strong Clergy and Community Councils to support and monitor local Police Operations.

• Improve public safety in and around schools, houses of worship and commercial areas.

• Promote youth legal education programs.

• Fully fund an independent Civilian Complaint Review Board.

• Permanently empower an independent City Commission like the Mollen Commission, to fight police corruption.

• Establish a Special Prosecutor to handle Police Brutality cases.

• Federal, state and city elected officials and justice agencies should conduct Public Hearings, and act on findings of police corruption, brutality, prison violence and related racial and criminal justice issues.

• Enact and enforce city, state and federal anti-bias laws with respect to civilians as well as law enforcement.

•   Adequately fund and fully operationalize the State Division of Human Rights, City Commission on Human Rights, Equal Employment Practices Commission, Division of Financial and Economic Opportunity, and Voter Assistance Commission.

•   Monitor, defeat and roll back, any federal, state and city legislation which results in disproportionate criminalization and incarceration of Blacks and Latinos.

•   Increase Black and Latino participation in law enforcement professions, including as prosecutors and judges.

•   Challenge the media, white and non-white, to project more positive portrayals of Blacks and Latinos, than the present stereotypes of criminality. Challenge media to refrain from exploiting public fears about crime.

•   Provide Blacks and Latinos greater economic opportunities in the criminal justice industry: construction contracts and jobs; entry level apprenticeships, mid- and senior-level employment; and contracts for goods and services. With appropriate community consultation and concurrence, locate prison facilities in or near minority neighborhoods.

•   Provide equal justice for all criminals, regardless of race. Recent federal sentencing guidelines for crack versus powder cocaine, with racially disparate impacts, are a classsic example to the contrary. If white criminals were incarcerated in closer proportion to their actual criminality, American society and its policymakers would probably become more sensitive to the need for prisoner rehabilitation, improved education, job training and opportunities, and other efforts to eliminate some of the root causes of crime.

References

American Civil Liberties Union Briefer, 1994, "10 Reasons to Oppose 3 Strikes You're Out."

Atlas of Crime and Justice In New York City, 1993, Vera Institute of Justice.

Beckett, Katherine, 1994 "Setting the Public Agenda:' Street Crime' and Drug Use in American Politics." *Social Problems*. 1(3):425-447.

Bell, Derrick, 1987, *And We Are Not Saved: The Elusive Quest for Racial Justice*, New York: Basic Books.

Center for Law and Social Justice, 1989, *Police and Racial Violence: Fact Versus Fiction*, Medgar Evers College, CUNY.

Chambliss, William, 1991, *Trading Textbooks for Prison Cells*. National Center on Institutions and Alternatives, VA.

Coffman, Edward M., 1994, "Dwight D.Eisenhower," Encarta, Microsoft and Funk & Wagnall's Corp.

Congressional Research Service and Library of Congress, 1995, via internet and world wide web, 104th Congress, "Contract With America" crime bill summaries.

Cook, Fred J., 1969, *The Warfare State*, New York: Collier Books.

Criminal Justice Research Committee, "Embryonic Signs of the Police State: The Implications of Six GOP Crime Bills on Blacks, Working Class and Most Americans, Backgrounder #3," Congr'l Black Caucus Fndn., Mar. 7, 1995.

Crutchfield, Robert, Bridges, George and Pitchford, Susan, 1994, "Crime, Social Structure and Criminal Punishment: White and Nonwhite Rates of Imprisonment."

Democratic Study Group, Fact Sheet No. 103-45, Nov. 28, 1994. (Omnibus Crime Bill analysis)

Ellis, Eddie, 1990, "Developing an Afro-Centric Model For Social Change: A Criminal Justice Discussion Paper (Unpublished)

_____, 1988. "Non-Traditional Approaches to Criminal and Social Justice: A Working Concept Paper." (Unpublished)

Federal Bureau of Investigation, *Uniform Crime Reports, 1991 and 1994.*

Forde, Yolande, 1995, *Caribbean People Under the Control of the Criminal Justice System in New York State*, Caribbean Research Center, Medgar Evers College, CUNY.

Franklin, John Hope, 1980, *From Slavery To Freedom*, New York: Alfred Knopf, Inc.

Georges-Abeyie, Daniel Ed, "The Criminal Justice System and Blacks," 1989, *Social Justice* 16(4):35-54.

Gordon, Diana R. et. al., 1992, "Urban Crime Policy," *Journal of Urban Affairs*, Vol. 14: 359-375.

Greer, Edward, 1978 - "The Class Nature of the Urban Policing during the period of Black Municipal Power," *Crime and Social Justice* (Spring-Summer):49-61; (Response to Critique pp. 70-71).

Hacker, Andrew, 1992, *Two Nations: Black and White, Separate, Hostile, Unequal.* New York: Charles Scribner's Sons.

_____, 1988 "Black Crime: White Racism," *New York Review* (MAR. 3): 36-41.

Hagan. 1974, "Extra Legal Attributes and Criminal Sentencing," *Law and Society Review* 8:357-83

Hatchett, David, 1990 "Equal Justice under the Law." *Crisis* 98 (4:12-17, 46).

Higginbotham, Jr., A. Leon, 1978, *In The Matter Of Color, Race & The American Legal Process: The Colonial Period.* New York: Oxford University Press.

Kleck, 1981 "Racial Discrimination in Criminal
    Sentencing." *American Sociological Review*. 46:
    783 - 805

Lovell and Pope. 1991 "Discrimination or No
    Discrimination: Methodological Critique of
    Evidence." *The Critical Criminologist*. 3(2)
    Summer.

Mauer, Marc, 1994 (Sept). "Americans Behind Bars:
    The International Use of Incarceration, 1992-
    1993." Sentencing Project, Wash., DC.

National Law Journal, "Major changes in the System
    favored by Juvenile Court Judges." 16 (49) 1, 24
    August 8, 1994.

Nelson J.F., 1991 "Racial and Ethnic Disparities in
    Processing Persons Arrested for Misdemeanor
    Crimes: New York State 1985 - 1986" Albany,
    NY: Division of Criminal Justice Services.

_____, 1992 "Hidden Disparities in Case Processing:
    New York State, 1985-1986." *Journal of Criminal
    Justice*. 20: 145-60.

NYC Dept. of City Planning, *Annual Report on Social
    Indicators, 1990 & 1993*.

NYC Dept. of Corrections, "Statistical Background, FY
    1994 (fact sheet)."

NYC Equal Employment Practices Commission, *1993 Annual Report.*

NYS Assembly Ways and Means Committee, "Statistical and Narrative Summary," Executive Budget, SFY 1995-96." (Criminal Justice agencies)

NYS Council On Children & Families, 1988, *Report on Juvenile Justice Issues.*

NYS Defenders Assoc., "Revised and Updated Memorandum Concerning A.7881," (Increased Sentencing for Violent Offenders), May 31, 1995.

NYS Dept. of Correctional Services, "Characteristics of Commitments, 1992;"and other statistical data.

NYS Division of Criminal Justice Services, *1990 Crime and Justice Annual Report.*

NYS Office of Court Administration, *1994 Annual Report, Franklin H. Williams Judicial Commission On Minorities.*

_____, and Unified Court System, 1994, unpublished data.

NYS Senate Reports, "Weekly Legislative Highlights, 1994 and 1995," via Internet.

New York Red Book, 1991-92, Albany, NY.

New York Times, four part series of articles on Youth, Crime and Violence, May 15-18, 1995, p.A1.

New York Times, Fox Butterfield, "Serious Crime Falls For Third Year, but Experts Warn Against Seeing Trend," May 23, 1995, p.A-14.

New York Times Editorial, "To Albany: Don't Undermine the N.Y.P.D." p.A20, June 29,1995.

Pope and Leyerhman.1992. *Minorities and the Juvenile Justice System.* Rockville MD. U.S. Department of Justice, Office of Juvenile Delinquency Prevention, Juvenile Justice Clearing House.

Rashbaum, William and Juan Forero, "New York's Roughest?" p.A6; "Top Cop Nixed Brutality Unit Idea," p.A8. *Newsday,* April 9, 1995.

Richey Mann, Coramae, 1993, *Unequal Justice: Question of Color,* Bloomington, Indiana University Press.

Sampson and Laub - 1993 "Structural Variations in Juvenile Court Processing: Inequality, the Under-class and Social Control." *Law and Society Review.* 27(2): 285 - 311.

Sullivan, Mercer, 1989, Testimony before Select Committee Hearing on Children, Youth and Families, U.S.House of Representatives (July 25th, pp. 106-109).

US Attorney General's Office, "Memorandum on the Omnibus Crime Control Act of 1994," Sept. 15, 1994, Wash. DC.

US Bureau of The Census, *Population Reports 1990*.

US Department of Justice, *Bureau of Justice Statistics*, 1991.

Walker, Samuel and K.B. Turner, "A Decade of Modest Progress: Employment of Black and Hispanic Police Officers, 1983-1992," Dept. of Criminal Justice, University of Nebraska, October 1993.

Zata, M. 1987, "The Changing Racial/Ethnic Biases in Sentencing." *Journal Of Research   in Crime and Delinquency*. 24(1): 69-92.

Appendix A:

Supplementary Figures and Tables

Inmate Recidivisim in New York

DBC
DuBois Bunche Center for Public Policy   MEDGAR EVERS COLLEGE, C.U.N.Y.

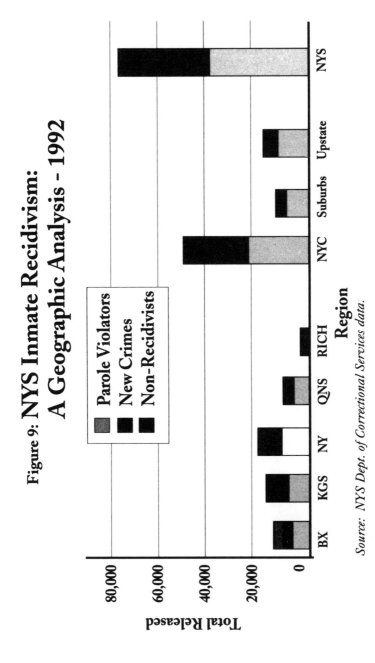

Figure 9: **NYS Inmate Recidivism: A Geographic Analysis - 1992**

Source: NYS Dept. of Correctional Services data.

Table 6 NYS Inmate Recidivism:
by Race & Type of Offense, 1980

1980	Releases	Recidivists	Type of Offense			
			New Crimes		Parole Violaters	
	(Col.1)	(Col.2)	(Col. 3)		(Col. 4)	
Blacks	3,818	1,719	45.0%	954	25.0%	785	20.6%
Whites	2,293	782	34.1%	390	17.0%	372	16.2%
Latinos	1,508	678	45.0%	353	23.4%	325	21.6%
Other	45	14	31.1%	7	15.6%	7	15.6%
Total	7,664	3,193	41.7%	1,704	22.2%	1,489	19.4%

Note: Col. 2 = Col. 3 + Col. 4
Source: NYS Dept. of Correctional Services data.

Table 7: Inmate Recidivism: A New York City Analysis – 1992

Region	Releases	Recidivists		Type of Offense New Crimes		Parole Violaters	
	(Col.1)	(Col.2)		(Col. 3)		(Col. 4)	
Bronx	11,342	5,227	46.1%	2,875	25.3%	2,352	20.7%
Kings	13,866	6,655	48.0%	3,663	26.4%	2,992	21.6%
New York	20,383	9,830	48.2%	5,156	25.3%	4,674	22.9%
Queens	7,846	3,742	47.7%	2,159	27.5%	1,583	20.2%
Richmond	778	356	45.8%	234	30.1%	122	15.7%
NYC Total	54,215	25,810	47.6%	14,087	26.0%	11,723	21.6%

Note: Suburban Region = Nassau, Suffolk, Westchester, and Rockland Counties
Source: *NYS Dept. of Correctional Services data.*

Table 8: NYS Inmate Recidivism: A New York State Analysis -1992

Region	Releases	Recidivists		Type of Offense			
				New Crimes		Parole Violators	
NYC Total	54,215	25,810	47.6%	14,087	26.0%	11,723	21.6%
Suburban	9,890	3,923	39.7%	2,215	22.4%	1,713	17.3%
Other NYS	16,770	6,863	40.9%	3,114	18.6%	3,749	22.4%
NYS Total	80,875	36,596	45.3%	19,416	24.0%	17,185	21.2%

Note: Suburban Region = Nassau, Suffolk, Westchester, and Rockland Counties
Source: NYS Dept. of Correctional Services data.

Appendix B:

Information Section

The DuBois Bunche Center
For Public Policy
Medgar Evers College, C.U.N.Y.

The DuBois Bunche Center For Public Policy
Office of the President, Medgar Evers College
The City University Of New York

The DuBois Bunche Center for Public Policy was founded in 1991 by Dr. Edison O. Jackson, the President of Medgar Evers College. It is named for two distinguished African-Americans who were world citizens, scholars, activists and statesmen, William Edward Burghardt DuBois and Ralph Johnson Bunche. Among their stellar achievements, DuBois and Bunche were pioneering scholars on the conditions of Black people in America. In their tradition, the DuBois Bunche Center's vision is to become a premier urban policy think tank, addressing the public policy concerns of Black and Latino New Yorkers and the broader community.

The DuBois Bunche Center's mission is to produce leading edge research and analysis, develop new paradigms and make incisive policy recommendations, which help policymakers and civic leadership address critical urban policy issues. The DuBois Bunche Center's fundamental goal is to impact upon the policy arena in order to improve the quality of urban life for New York's Black and Latino communities and beyond.

The DuBois Bunche Center conducts policy, legislative and budgetary research; and presents its policy studies, findings and reports to legislators, policy makers, public administrators and community leaders. The DuBois Bunche Center collaborates with faculty, students, scholars, researchers, practitioners, think tanks, key institutions and community leaders, engaging in vigorous discourse and critical analysis, in order to frame issues in incisive conceptual frameworks and to formulate substantive solutions to pressing urban problems.

The DuBois Bunche Center's policy research and activities have included substantive areas such as health care, urban education, welfare reform, children and families, criminal and juvenile justice; capacity building issues around the Black church, community and economic development, and information technology; governmental processes such as public budgeting, policy-making, voting rights and redistricting; and intergroup relations and multicultural issues. The DuBois Bunche Center utilizes the internet, world wide web, and other state-of-the-art technologies in its research activities. It maintains a print and electronic reference library for use by the academic and broader community and serves as an information clearinghouse. The DuBois Bunche Center collaborates on conferences, seminars, workshops and symposia; produces research publications; and conducts media outreach and education through its "Public Policy Roundtable" segment, which airs on television, cable and radio stations.

The DuBois Bunche Center staff and researchers carry out faculty assignments; serve as policy and technical advisors, and serve in senior appointive positions in the academic, public and private sector arenas. The DuBois Bunche Center is a university based, non-profit, non-partisan research organization, whose Board of Advisors, is chaired by Dr. Edison O. Jackson, and it includes federal, state and city legislators and public officials, as well as distinguished academicians, policy makers and community leaders.

W. E. B. DuBois

William Edward Burghardt DuBois was born of humble origins in Great Barrington, Massachusetts in 1868.   He completed his undergraduate education at Fisk University; and received Bachelor's and Master's degrees from Harvard University. In 1896, he received his Ph.D. in Philosophy from Harvard University, with a doctoral dissertation entitled, " The Suppression of the African Slave Trade to the United States of America, 1638-1870;" and he did post-doctoral studies at the University of Berlin.

DuBois served on the faculties of Wilberforce University and the University of Pennsylvania, where he researched *The Philadelphia Negro*, America's first sociological study of an urban Black community. He was appointed professor of history and economics; and for twenty years, produced the "Atlanta University Studies of the Negro Problem," the definitive body of sociological research on Blacks in America. W.E.B. DuBois was a founder of the Niagara Movement, the N.A.A.C.P. and editor of its *Crisis* magazine.   He was also a founder of the Pan African Congress, which birthed African nations' independence from European colonialism   W.E.B. Du Bois, one of the world's great scholars, intellectuals and international activists, died in Accra, Ghana on August 27, 1963, at the dawn of the March On Washington.

Sources: David L. Lewis, *W.E.B. Du Bois Biography Of A Race, 1868 - 1919*. Henry Holt and Company, Inc. New York, 1993.; Mark Stafford, *W.E.B. Du Bois Scholar And Activist*. Chelsea House Publishers. New York, 1989.

Ralph Bunche

Ralph Johnson Bunche was born of humble origins in Detroit, Michigan in 1904. He graduated summa cum laude and was class valedictorian at the University of California at Los Angeles. He received his Master's degree in Political Science; and his Ph.D. in Government and International Relations, from Harvard University, with the year's best doctoral dissertation entitled, "French Administration in Togo and Dahomey." Bunche founded the Political Science Department at Howard University; produced several scholarly works on urban Black America, politics, race and international relations; and he was a major contributor to Gunnar Myrdal's *An American Dilemna*, a classic work on America's race relations.

Ralph Bunche headed the Africa Section of the U.S. Office of Strategic Services during World War II. He was one of America's key strategists in the formation of the United Nations; was the first African-American to receive the Nobel Peace Prize in 1950 for the Arab - Israeli settlement; was a major architect of the decolonialization of Africa; and was a behind-the-scenes supporter of the American Civil Rights movement. This great international statesman and scholar served as Under Secretary for Political Affairs at the United Nations until his death in 1971.

Sources:Brian Urquhart, *Ralph Bunche An American Life*. W.W. Norton And Company. New York, 1993.; Benjamin Rivlin, Editor, *Ralph Bunche The Man And His Times*. Holmes & Meier Publishers, Inc. New York, 1990.

The DuBois Bunche Center for Public Policy
Medgar Evers College, City University Of New York

The Board of Advisors

Dr. Edison O Jackson,President
Medgar Evers College, CUNY
Chairman of the Board of Advisors

Hon. Howard Dodson, Chief
Schomburg Center for Research in Black Culture

Dr. Pamela Reid, Associate Provost
& Dean of Academic Affairs
CUNY Graduate Center

Dr. Megan McLaughlin, Executive Director/CEO
Federation of Protestant Welfare Agencies

U S. Congressman Edolphus Towns
10th C.D., Brooklyn, NY

U.S. Congressman Major Owens
11th C.D., Brooklyn, N.Y.

Dr. Preston Wilcox, Chairman
AFRAM Associates

Dr. George Irish, Executive Director,
Caribbean Research Center
Medgar Evers College, CUNY

Dr. Rafael Zambrana,
School of Business & Public Administration
Medgar Evers College, CUNY

The Board of Advisors (continued)

Hon. Albert Vann, Chair
Corporations, Authorities & Commissions Committee
New York State Assembly

Hon. Edward Griffith
Assistant Speaker
New York State Assembly

Hon. Mary Pinkett, Chair
Governmental Operations Committee
New York City Council

Hon. Clarence Norman, Jr.
Assistant Majority Leader
New York State Assembly

Hon. Roger Green, Chair
Children & Families Committee
New York State Assembly

Hon. Una Clarke, Chair
Mental Health Subcommittee
New York City Council

Dr. Louis DeFreitas, Sr.
Educator and Journalist

Hon. Marty Markowitz
New York State Senator

Dr. Carlos Russell
Dept. of Interdisciplinary Studies
Medgar Evers College, CUNY

The Board of Advisors (continued)

Dr. Esmeralda Simmons, Executive Director
Center For Law and Social Justice
Medgar Evers College, CUNY

Hon. James Conolly, Director
Alternative Sentencing Program
Kings County District Attorney's Office

John Flateau, Executive Director
DuBois Bunche Center For Public Policy
Medgar Evers College, CUNY

A Public Policy Trilogy

of the

DuBois Bunche Center For Public Policy
Medgar Evers College, CUNY

Young Lives, American Dreams

($ 18.95 retail, plus shipping & handling)

The Prison Industrial Complex

($ 13.95 retail , plus shipping & handling)

Blackout ? Media Ownership Concentration

($ 26.95 retail, plus shipping and handling)

Order today ! Call *1-800-247-6553,*
- or visit our website:
http://www.atlasbooks.com/marktplc/00821.htm
(<u>Bulk</u> Discounts Available !)